Busy Kids®
Busy Days
Fall & Winter

Table of Contents

©2002 by THE EDUCATION CENTER, INC.
All rights reserved.

ISBN #1-56234-511-7

Except as provided for herein, no part of this publication may be reproduced or transmitted in any form or by any means, electronic or mechanical, including photocopying, recording, or storing in any information storage and retrieval system or electronic online bulletin board, without prior written permission from The Education Center, Inc. Permission is given to the original purchaser to reproduce patterns and reproducibles for individual classroom use only and not for resale or distribution. Reproduction for an entire school or school system is prohibited. Please direct written inquiries to The Education Center, Inc., P.O. Box 9753, Greensboro, NC 27429-0753. The Education Center®, *The Mailbox*®, Busy Kids®, and the mailbox/post/grass logo are trademarks of The Education Center, Inc., and may be the subject of one or more federal trademark registrations. All other brand or product names are trademarks or registered trademarks of their respective companies.

Manufactured in the United States
10 9 8 7 6 5 4 3

About This Book

Once featured as the popular Busy Kids® series, the contents of these eight great books have been restructured into two new books that make planning your theme-based units even easier! *Busy Kids Busy Days—Fall & Winter* and *Busy Kids Busy Days—Spring & Summer* will help you present complete theme units that feature the curriculum you need to fill your busy kids' days. Each theme unit is divided into several two-page sections featuring ideas for the following learning categories.

ABCs & 123s: Provide your little ones with the building blocks for school success with the ideas featured on the ABCs & 123s pages. You'll find fun and creative ideas for teaching basic concepts and building basic skills, such as letters, numbers, colors, shapes, counting, graphing, patterning, and much more!

Centers: These useful Centers pages present ideas for enhancing traditional centers and for creating easy-to-set-up thematic centers. Each idea reinforces skills while providing fun learning opportunities for children with different learning styles.

Circle Time: In the Circle Time section, you'll find helpful strategies and creative activities for one of the most essential segments of the preschool or kindergarten child's school day. Each original activity has been developed to focus on early childhood skills and concepts in inviting and playful ways.

Fine Motor: The ideas featured in the Fine Motor section provide big ideas for those little hands! You'll see crafts, centers, fingerplays, recipes, and skill-building ideas for language, science, and math. And each of those great ideas helps youngsters develop their small-muscle strength and coordination in fun and creative ways.

Movement: The Movement section features age-appropriate movement activities designed for indoor and outdoor play, and many require only minimal equipment. With these fun-to-use ideas, you're sure to watch your students' gross-motor skills improve by leaps and bounds!

Snacktime: The Snacktime pages feature clever recipes using an easy step-by-step format. Each recipe can be followed from start to finish with little or no help from the teacher. What a fun way to build youngsters' self-confidence! You'll be mixing important skills into your snacktime as youngsters develop their small-muscle coordination and work on measurement, counting, language skills, and much more.

We've conveniently made the recipe pages reproducible so you can copy, color, and laminate each one before placing it in your cooking area. Each recipe features a bonus idea to help you make the most of extra ingredients and add an extra helping of learning to your lesson.

Songs & Rhymes: Turn to the Songs & Rhymes section to find plenty of fingerplays, action rhymes, and songs sung to popular tunes—just right for little learners. Plus, you'll find many accompanying activities with puppets, games, and props to help you introduce concepts and reinforce skills.

Storytime: Check out the suggested books and literature-based ideas the Storytime section has to offer. Five story recommendations for every theme provide lots of age-appropriate picture books to share. And, for each selection, you'll get a fresh idea for integrating learning and literature.

Family

Parade of Homes

There's much to learn when you address the different types of homes in which families live. Discuss with youngsters the many different types of homes, such as houses, mobile homes, and apartments. Then encourage each child to draw a picture of his home. (Or have younger children bring in photos of their homes.) Mount each child's drawing on a piece of tagboard; then write his address under his drawing. Then label a separate envelope with each child's address. Place the drawings and envelopes in a center. To use, a student pair spreads the drawings out on a table. Each partner then matches an envelope to the appropriate address. The pair continues until all the matches have been made. Then each child finds his drawing and recites his address to his partner.

123 East 12th Street
Apt. 4B

123 East 12th Street
Apt. 4B

Home Is Where the Hearts Are

Get to the heart of the matter by teaching little ones that families come in many different shapes and sizes. To begin, cut out a simple construction paper house for each child. Then cut out an ample supply of large and small hearts from construction paper. Have each child label a small heart for each child in her family and a large heart for each adult. Have her glue the hearts onto her house cutout. Then ask her to add features to each heart—such as a head, arms, and legs—to represent the corresponding family member. Collect the houses; then put them in a center. Invite visitors to sort the houses by the number of family members, the number of adults, or the number of children.

Family Footwork

Step into family fun with this home-school project. Send each child home with a few large sheets of construction paper in one color. (If possible, send a different color to each family.) Include a note explaining that the child will trace and cut out one foot (or shoe) outline of each family member. Ask that one member help the child label the cutouts with the appropriate person's name. Back in class, have each youngster count the foot cutouts in his collection and then sequence the cutouts by size. Then divide your class into student pairs. Invite the partners to combine their cutouts and then sequence them by size. As they work together, encourage the students to determine if any of their family members have the same foot size. Which member has the largest foot? The smallest foot? Now that's some fancy footwork!

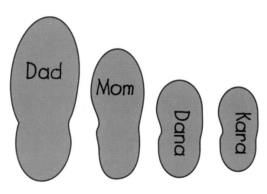

Family Rap

"Rap" your youngsters in family pride with this alphabet chant. After your little ones learn the chant, have half the class chant the letters while the other half recites the lines. Then switch parts and wrap up this activity with another go-round.

A - B - CDE
In a family is the place for me!
F - G - HIJ
Families work and families play.
K - L - MNO
My family's love helps me grow.
P - Q - RST
Family makes me so happy.
U - V - WXY
Family makes me smile with pride.
Z - Z - ZZZ
I sure love my family!

Family Names

Family names are passed along from generation to generation. Recognize youngsters' family names as you pass along some counting practice with this idea. To prepare, identify the child in your class with the longest last name. Count the letters in his last name; then write the numerals from 1 to that number along the bottom of your chalkboard to create a number graph. Then help each child write (or trace over) his last name on a sentence strip. Have him count the letters in his name; then have him tape his name strip above the corresponding numeral on the chalkboard. When the graph is complete, have the class count the names in each column and discuss the results.

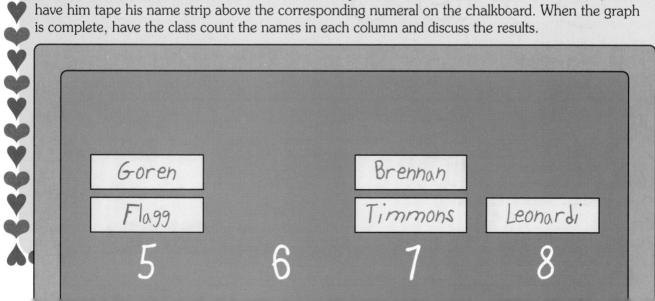

Family

Mommy's Purse

Stuff a center with some of the treasures usually found stuffed in Mommy's purse! Gather a large purse, a wallet, keys, a pair of sunglasses, a comb, a notepad, a pen, and other items typically found in a pocketbook. Draw or trace each item on a tagboard card. Tape the cards to a table; then place each item in a separate sock and knot the end of the sock. Put the socks in the purse.

When a child visits this center, she removes a sock from the purse, feels its contents, and then places the sock on the card she believes matches its contents. After she empties the purse, she may empty the socks to check her guesses. Then she repacks each sock and repacks the purse so another curious youngster can discover the treasures in Mommy's purse.

Home Away From Home

Invite your little ones to create a dream home away from home in your block center. Encourage youngsters to construct a house of blocks. Provide toy people and doll furniture, and invite your little interior decorators to attach fabric-square curtains and carpet to the house to give it that homey feel. And don't forget to provide a toy cat or dog for the family pet. You might even suggest that youngsters build a doghouse for the dog. Everyone is sure to feel right at home in this center!

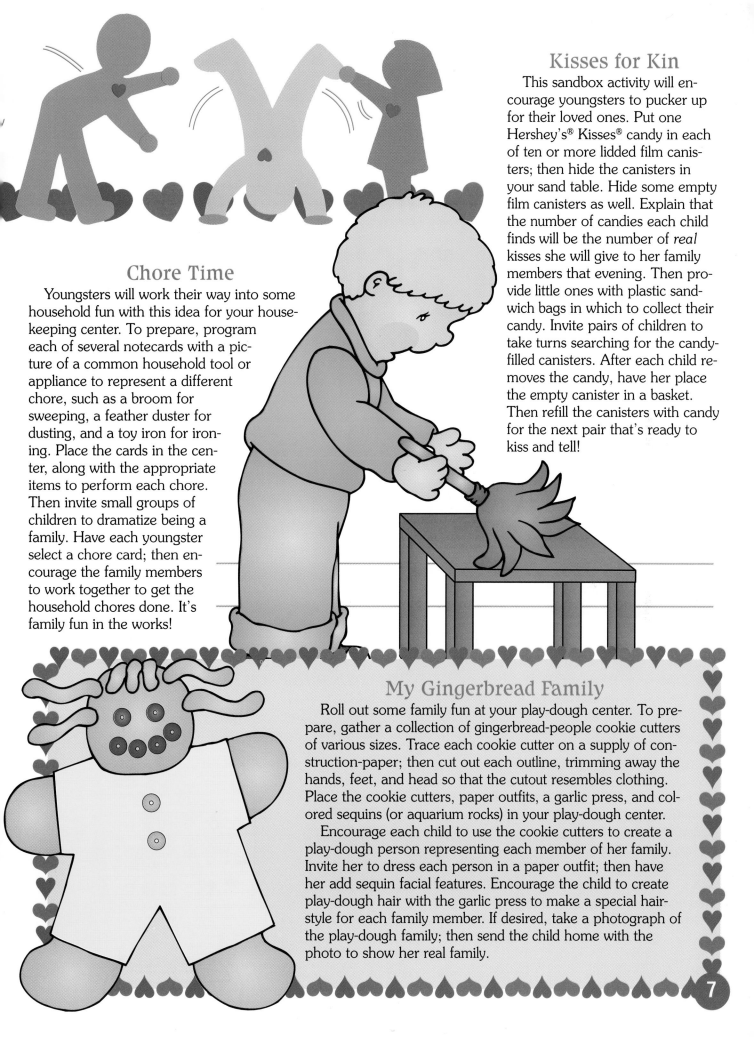

Kisses for Kin

This sandbox activity will encourage youngsters to pucker up for their loved ones. Put one Hershey's® Kisses® candy in each of ten or more lidded film canisters; then hide the canisters in your sand table. Hide some empty film canisters as well. Explain that the number of candies each child finds will be the number of *real* kisses she will give to her family members that evening. Then provide little ones with plastic sandwich bags in which to collect their candy. Invite pairs of children to take turns searching for the candy-filled canisters. After each child removes the candy, have her place the empty canister in a basket. Then refill the canisters with candy for the next pair that's ready to kiss and tell!

Chore Time

Youngsters will work their way into some household fun with this idea for your housekeeping center. To prepare, program each of several notecards with a picture of a common household tool or appliance to represent a different chore, such as a broom for sweeping, a feather duster for dusting, and a toy iron for ironing. Place the cards in the center, along with the appropriate items to perform each chore. Then invite small groups of children to dramatize being a family. Have each youngster select a chore card; then encourage the family members to work together to get the household chores done. It's family fun in the works!

My Gingerbread Family

Roll out some family fun at your play-dough center. To prepare, gather a collection of gingerbread-people cookie cutters of various sizes. Trace each cookie cutter on a supply of construction-paper; then cut out each outline, trimming away the hands, feet, and head so that the cutout resembles clothing. Place the cookie cutters, paper outfits, a garlic press, and colored sequins (or aquarium rocks) in your play-dough center.

Encourage each child to use the cookie cutters to create a play-dough person representing each member of her family. Invite her to dress each person in a paper outfit; then have her add sequin facial features. Encourage the child to create play-dough hair with the garlic press to make a special hairstyle for each family member. If desired, take a photograph of the play-dough family; then send the child home with the photo to show her real family.

Family

We eat spaghetti at my house!

Mealtime Is Share Time

Gather together in a circle to share a tidbit or two about family mealtimes. Have your children pass a piece of play food around the circle as you recite the following poem. At the end of the verse, have the child holding the food item stand to share a story about a preferred family food, a mealtime custom, or a favorite mealtime story.

Oh, mealtime is sharing time;
We share food and stories and fun.
We talk and listen; eat and drink.
It's a great time for everyone!

You Can Always Count On Family

Count on family for fun! In advance cut a house shape from construction paper for each child—plus a few extras. Before circle time, ask each youngster to draw his family members "inside" a house. If a child splits his time between two residences, give him more than one house. Have him bring his drawing(s) to circle time to show and tell about his family. Then teach youngsters the following poem. Next begin counting and invite each youngster to stand when he hears the number that represents his family. Invite comparisons. Who has the smallest family? The largest?

How many people in your family?
How many special to you?
Stand when you hear the right number.
Don't forget to include YOU!

Go Camping

Go to the Park

Work Puzzles

Star Entertainment

Find out what families do for fun and frolic. To prepare, cut a small construction-paper star for each child. At circle time, discuss with your youngsters what they do with their families for fun; then list their responses on the chalkboard (leave plenty of room between responses). Give each child a star to tape next to the type of entertainment he most enjoys with his family. If desired, stretch this activity over the course of a few days. On separate days, have the students use the stars to show their favorite family activities that take place indoors, outdoors, and while on vacation. It's fun for the whole family!

The Chore Challenge

Doing chores is one way of helping each other in a family. Help youngsters make a list of typical chores they do at home. From the list, vote on one chore that all the children could do to help their families. Decide on the number of days the chore is to be done. Then write a short parent note that states the designated chore and the number of days the children have agreed to do it. Include a line for parents to sign when the chore is completed. Ask students to return the signed notes to school at the end of the designated period. Then watch your youngsters "chore-tle" with delight as you award them with ribbons for a task well done!

Family Love Song

Sing this loving song with your children to underscore the key element of families—love. Once youngsters have learned the words to the song, have them sing it for their families at home.

You Are My Family
(sung to the tune of "You Are My Sunshine")

You are my family, my loving family.
I feel so happy living with you.
You are so special, so very special!
Thanks for loving me the way you do.

Teach this second verse to show your little ones that your class is a special family, too.

You are my family, my preschool family,
I feel so happy right here with you.
With you I play, sing, and learn so many things.
Thanks for loving me the way you do.

Family

Family Trees

These special trees are sure to become family keepsakes. In advance, ask parents to send a photo of their child's immediate family to school. (Inform parents that the photo will not be returned.) Cut out the faces of each child's family members; then put them in an envelope labeled with the child's name.

To make a family tree, a child traces a six-inch circle onto green construction paper and a 4" x 7" rectangle onto brown construction paper; then he cuts out the shapes. He glues his cutouts onto a sheet of white paper to make a tree. Then he sponge-paints a red apple for each of his family members. When the paint dries, he glues the photo of each family member onto an apple. Then he glues his own face cutout near the base of the tree and draws his body. Help each child write "I couldn't have picked a better family!" near his photo to complete his project.

Luke's family

I couldn't have picked a better family!

Lovable Family Pets

Dog-ear this idea—it's the "purr-fect" family pet activity! Give each child a nine-inch construction-paper square. Show her how to fold the square in half to create a triangle. Then have her open her square and cut along the fold to make two triangles. Invite her to convert her triangles into family pets with a few simple folds. To create a puppy, have the child fold the two corners of the long side of the triangle down to make puppy ears. To make pointy kitten ears, have her fold the corners up. Invite each child to draw facial features on each of her pets; then have her glue a craft-stick handle to each one. Now youngsters have a lovable litter of puppies and kittens!

Full Hearts

Invite little ones to give a piece of their hearts to their loved ones with these family puzzles. To prepare, gather a class supply of small manila envelopes. Then, for each child, cut a large heart from tagboard. Working with two or three students at a time, ask each youngster to count the number of people in his family, including himself. On each child's heart, draw lines to create a section for each family member; then help the child write each family member's name in a separate section. Then invite him to color the heart as he desires. Have him cut the heart apart on the lines. Then ask him to write his name on an envelope before putting the puzzle pieces inside, along with a copy of this poem. Invite him to take his puzzle home for his family to assemble.

Each member of my family
Is so very dear to me.
Each holds a place within my heart,
As you will surely see.

Family Flags

Your little ones will wave these personalized flags with family pride. In advance, write each child's last name in uppercase letters on a separate piece of 4 1/2" x 12" tagboard. Then collect a class supply of plastic straws. Place the tagboard flags and straw flagpoles in a center, along with glue, glitter, star stickers, and a stapler.

To make a flag, a child traces each letter of her last name with glue; then she sprinkles glitter over the glue. She decorates her flag with star stickers, and then staples a straw to the left side of her flag. Encourage your youngsters to take their fantastic family flags home to display with pride and joy.

Hugs and Kisses

Little ones can shower their families with hugs and kisses as they explore the symbols X and O. To begin, show youngsters each symbol; then explain its meaning. Invite each child to practice drawing these two symbols. Then show students how to draw their families using these symbols. On your chalkboard, draw a hugs-and-kisses person as shown. Then invite little ones to draw their own hugs-and-kisses people and to label each one with a family member's name. Encourage each child to present his special illustration to his real-life family, accompanied by a real-life hug and kiss for each family member.

11

Family

Family Circle

Circle around for some family fun with this home-style version of "The Farmer in the Dell." Discuss with your little ones how a family is like a circle of love. Talk about the people who make up a family. Form a circle; then have each child select a family role. Ask any child role-playing a mother to stand in the center of the circle; then circle around the mothers as you sing along to the following song. As you invite additional children into the circle, substitute the names of the family members they are pretending to be.

A Circle of Love
(sung to the tune of "The Farmer in the Dell")

A circle of love,
A circle of love,
A family is just like a circle of love.
Our family has some [moms].
Our family has some [moms].
Come and see our family,
Our family has some [moms].

Final verse:
Our circle is complete.
Our family is so neat.
We all are here.
Let's give a cheer!
Our circle is complete.

Chores Galore

Have you ever seen a child ask to do a chore? It's guaranteed with this mother's helper version of Mother, May I? Begin by talking about the kinds of chores children do to help out at home. Then have your youngsters line up on one side of the play area while you—the mother—go to the opposite side. Ask one child at a time to do a chore, such as set the table, make the bed, feed the pet, etc. Instruct each child to ask permission by saying, "Mother, May I?" Grant permission and indicate the number of steps each child can go forward. As each child takes his steps, encourage him to role-play the chore. Continue the game until a child taps you and exclaims, "The chores are all done!" Don't be surprised if youngsters ask for another round of chores!

Counting On Family

Help your students catch on to the fact that families come in all different sizes. First review the number of people in each child's immediate family. Then organize your little ones into a large semi-circle. Stand facing them with a basket of ten or more scarves. Call out, "Who has four people in his or her family?" Count to four, then use both hands to toss the scarves into the air. Encourage each child who has four family members to rush into the circle and catch one of the scarves. Change the number you call out each time. Who has the most family members? It's a toss-up!

Family Pass

Here's an activity your students won't want to pass up! Ask your little ones to sit one behind the other on the floor; then pretend you are a family playing together. Give a ball to the first child in line. (A large sponge ball works best.) Instruct him to hold the ball with both hands and pass it over his head to the person behind him. Continue passing the ball until it reaches the end of the line. As the last child in line calls out, "I'm sending it back," he must pass the ball to the child sitting in front of him and run to the front of the line before the ball gets there. When the ball is back where it started, pass along the family fun all over again!

Riding Round the Town

Hop in for a rollicking ride in the family car! First discuss the places in town that your students like to visit with their families. Then create a family car to travel to those places. Arrange the children in two parallel lines; then ask each child to put his outer hand on the shoulder of the person standing in front of him. Have the child at the head of each line hold onto your waist. Using a pot lid for a steering wheel, lead the car full of kiddies around the town. Vary the speed at which you drive, encouraging the car to move as a unit. Sing the following song together as you stop at some favorite family spots.

Our Family Car
(sung to the tune of "Bumping Up and Down")

Bumping up and down in our family car.   *Move bodies up and down.*

Bumping up and down in our family car.
Bumping up and down in our family car.
Where will we go this morning?

Other verses:
Going around the corner in our family car…   *Take a sharp turn.*
Going down the hill in our family car…   *Increase speed.*
Stopping at the light in our family car…   *Stand in place.*

13

Family

House Full of Love

Ingredients:
1 1/2 slices of bread per child
peanut butter
raisins
1 Hershey's® Kisses® candy per child

Utensils and Supplies:
1 plastic knife (or craft stick) per child
heart-shaped cookie cutter
napkins
knife

Teacher Preparation:
   Remove the crust from each slice of bread. Cut the necessary number of bread slices in half (diagonally). Arrange the ingredients and utensils near the step-by-step direction cards.

What to Do When the Snack Is Through

   You're bound to have sweet success with this activity that provides practice with patterning and ordinal numbers. Distribute an equal number of the leftover Hershey's® Kisses® and raisins. Have your own supply handy. Create a pattern, such as *candy, raisin, candy, raisin.* Have youngsters copy or extend your pattern, or encourage them to create their own patterns. Then have each youngster unwrap his candies and put them in a row. Have him line up his raisins separately. Give directions using ordinal numbers, such as, "Eat your third raisin," or "Eat your second Kiss." Vary the ordinal number and the food item until every morsel is eaten!

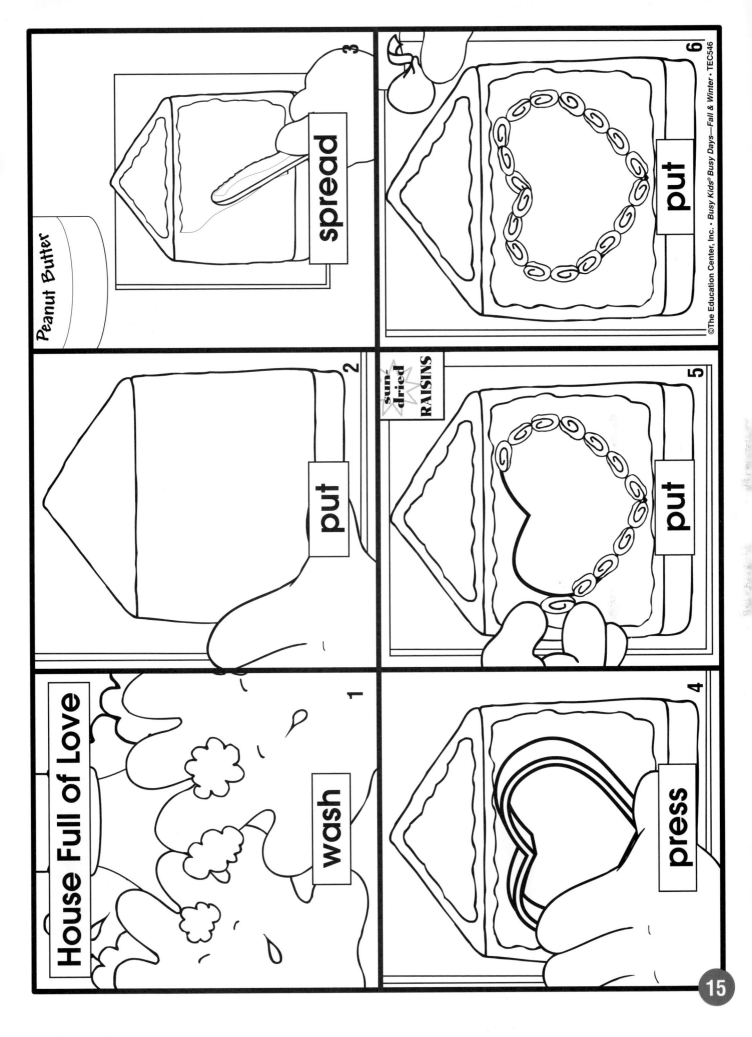

House Full of Love

1 — wash

2 — put

3 — spread

Peanut Butter

4 — press

5 — put

sun-dried RAISINS

6 — put

©The Education Center, Inc. • *Busy Kids® Busy Days—Fall & Winter* • TEC546

Family

All in the Family

Invite youngsters to sing this song about the most important people in their lives. To create additional verses, substitute other family members and the appropriate pronoun for the underlined words.

(sung to the tune of "My Bonnie Lies Over the Ocean")

My [mommy] is part of my family.
My [mommy] is someone I love.
My [mommy] is part of my family.
[She]'s someone that I love to love!

[Mommy, mommy],
Is very important to me, to me.
[Mommy, mommy],
[She]'s someone in my family.

Some people in my family are Burt and Janet...

Some People in My Family

Introduce little ones to this tune; then invite each child to fill in the names of her personal family members (such as brothers, sisters, grandparents, or pets) for the underlined words.

(sung to the tune of "The Wheels on the Bus")

Some people in my family are [Mom and Dad],
[Mom and Dad], [Mom and Dad].
Some people in my family are [Mom and Dad].
How I love them so!

Cheers for Family

(sung to the tune of "Zip-a-Dee-Do-Dah")

Zip-a-dee-do-dah, zip-a-dee-ay,
Let's cheer for our families!
 Hooray! Hooray!
Plenty of lovin' every day.
Zip-a-dee-do-dah, zip-a-dee-ay!

Sing a Song of Families

Ask each child to count the number of adults and the number of children in her family. Then sing this song, inserting a child's name and the appropriate numbers for her family. Each time you sing the song, use a different child's name.

(sung to the tune of "Sing a Song of Sixpence")

Let's sing a song of [Kelly]'s
Loving family.
[Two] grown-ups and [two] children
Make up [her] family.
When they get together,
They talk and eat and play.
They love each other very much
Each and every day!

Spending Time Together

Teach youngsters this poem about family togetherness. Then brainstorm other things that families do together. If desired, incorporate your youngsters' responses into the third line of the verse.

What do families like to do
When spending time together?
Talk and laugh and play and read—
Could anything be better?

17

Family

Alligator Baby

When Kristen's parents bring home her new baby brother, it isn't at all what she expected. Read Robert Munsch's hilarious tale *Alligator Baby* (Cartwheel Books); then teach your little ones this song that reviews the story's events. Invite two student volunteers to role-play the parents while the rest of the class pretends to be Kristen. Have the parents stand in front of the class and take turns holding a doll that is completely wrapped in a blanket until the final verse.

(sung to the tune of "He's Got the Whole World in His Hands")

They've got the alligator baby in their hands.
They've got the alligator baby in their hands.
They've got the alligator baby in their hands.
Now take it back to the zoo!   *Shake index finger and put other hand on hip.*

They've got the little seal baby in their hands....
They've got the little monkey baby in their hands....

They've got my little baby brother in their hands.
They've got my little baby brother in their hands.
They've got my little baby brother in their hands.
Now no more zoo for you!   *Shake index finger and put other hand on hip.*

Me and My Family Tree

Joan Sweeney's *Me and My Family Tree* (Crown Publishers, Inc.) provides a simple explanation of how children and their relatives are connected to each other. For a fun follow-up, invite youngsters to make these family treehouses. Set up your art center with a class supply of 4" x 6" house shapes cut from white construction paper; a nine-inch tagboard circle, a 3" x 6" tagboard rectangle, 9" x 12" construction paper in green, brown, and blue; markers; and glue.

A child at this center uses the tagboard patterns to trace and then cut out a green circle and a brown rectangle from construction paper. He forms a tree shape with his cutouts and glues the tree to a blue construction paper background. Next he draws each family member that he lives with on a house shape. He writes (or dictates) the names of his family members under the drawings. Then he glues the house shape to the tree to make a family treehouse.

The Relatives Came

What could be more fun than a summer spent with the relatives? After sharing the joyful fun of Cynthia Rylant's *The Relatives Came* (Aladdin Paperbacks), share these "related" verses to the story.

(sung to the tune of "You Are My Sunshine")

Oh, when the relatives, huggin'-
   kissin' relatives,
Came to visit all summer long,
Oh, there was eatin' and crowded
   sleepin',
When the relatives came along.

Oh, when the relatives, huggin'-
   kissin' relatives,
Came for a visit all summer long,
Oh, there was playin' and music
   makin',
When the relatives came along.

Oh, when the relatives, huggin'-
   kissin' relatives,
Left from their visit all summer long,
Oh, there was dreamin' 'bout the
   very next summer,
When the relatives come back along.

Horace

I love you, dear family.
I know you love me, too.
And if I could start over—
Choose a family anew—
You know you can be certain
That I would still choose you !

Horace by Holly Keller (Mulberry Books) is the tender tale of a little spotted leopard adopted into a family of striped tigers. The story celebrates the ties that bind families together. After reading it, invite youngsters to make these heart-shaped love poems for their families. First, copy the poem shown and duplicate it for each child. Make heart-shaped patterns from tagboard and place them at your art center along with the poem copies, construction paper, colorful curling ribbon, hole punchers, scissors, and tape.

To make a love poem, trace a heart pattern onto construction paper, cut it out, and then glue the poem to the heart. Punch holes around the outside of the heart. Tape one end of a length of curling ribbon to the back of the heart, and then lace the ribbon through the holes. Secure the ribbon by taping the loose end to the back side. Have each child take his love poem home to his one-of-a-kind family.

One Hundred Is a Family

Pam Muñoz Ryan embraces many different types of families—both traditional and nontraditional—in *One Hundred Is a Family* (Hyperion Press Limited). After sharing this cheerful counting book with your class, discuss how your classroom is a family connected by bonds of friendship. Then cut out a large schoolhouse shape from red bulletin board paper and mount it on a bulletin board. Give each child a sheet of white drawing paper and markers, and encourage her to draw a full-length picture of herself. Have her cut around her drawing and glue her picture to the schoolhouse. Invite any adults who work with your class to draw self-portraits, too. Once the pictures are glued to the schoolhouse, count together all the people in your class family and insert the number into the title "[Number] is a family sharing a classroom."

Leaves

Turn Over a New Leaf

Shape recognition and fun are a perfect match in this game. To prepare, cut 12 identical leaves from colored tagboard. Divide the leaves into pairs; then program each pair with one of the following shapes: circle, square, triangle, rectangle, diamond, or oval. Laminate the leaves for durability; then put them in a center and invite student pairs to play this memory game. To play, arrange the leaves facedown on a table. The first player turns over two leaves. She identifies the shapes on the leaves. If the shapes match, she keeps the pair. If the shapes do not match, she returns them to the play table. Then the next player takes her turn. The game continues until all the pairs are found.

Fall Leaf Countdown

Use this countdown chant to reinforce number skills. In advance, collect (or cut from construction paper) five leaves each for half the students in your class. Then divide your class into student pairs. Designate one child in each pair to be a tree and the other child to be the wind. Give each tree five leaves; then have the trees spread out in an open area of the room. Ask each tree to hold the leaves in his hands and then position his arms to resemble branches. Recite the chant. Each time you reach the word "Whoosh!" in the rhyme, have the wind puff and pull a leaf from the tree branch. After completing the chant, invite the partners to switch roles for another round of wind-blowing, leaf-falling excitement.

Five little fall leaves hanging on a tree,
Teasing the wind, "You can't catch me!"
Along comes the wind, strong as can be.
  Whoosh!
One little leaf falls from
  the tree.

Four little fall leaves…
Three little fall leaves…
Two little fall leaves…
One little fall leaf…

No little fall leaves hanging on a tree.
It sure looks like wintertime to me!

Whoosh!

Loose Leaf Toss

Positional words are "unbe-leaf-ably" easy to learn with this hands-on activity. In advance, cut out two construction paper leaves for each child. Use rope or yarn to make a circle in an open area of your room. Seat your class around the circle; then distribute the leaves evenly among the children. On a signal, have the children toss their leaves into the air. Once the leaves settle, chorally count the leaves that landed *in* the circle. Then count the leaves that are *out of* the circle. Where did most of the leaves land? Ask each youngster to retrieve two leaves. Place a chair in the circle; then signal students to toss their leaves again. This time count the leaves *on* the chair, *under* the chair, *in front of* the chair, and *behind* the chair, as well as those *outside* the circle.

Leaf Pile

Pile up some estimation skills with this activity. In advance, gather a supply of leaves in a variety of colors and sizes. (Or cut out a collection of construction paper leaves.) Pile a small amount of the leaves onto a paper plate. Show youngsters the leaf pile; then ask them to estimate the number of leaves on the plate. Have each child write his estimate on a sticky note labeled with his name. Then have him attach his sticky note to the chalkboard. Ask younger students to match the notes that have the same numerals. Have older students arrange the notes in numerical order. Then count the leaves in the pile. Did any of the students guess the correct number? Which students estimated more leaves? Fewer leaves? After comparing the results, create a new pile of leaves on the plate; then jump in for more estimating fun!

All Sorts of Fun

Bag those all-important observation skills with this leaf-sorting activity. To begin, select three leaf types that are indigenous to your area. For each child, collect (or cut from construction paper) at least one of each type. Gather three paper grocery bags; then glue a different leaf type on each bag. Label each bag with the corresponding tree name. Put the bags and leaves in a center. Invite small groups to sort the leaves into the bags.

If you have a variety of fallen leaves around your school's campus, try this follow-up activity. Give each child a paper bag and a leaf from your classroom; then take your class outdoors. Challenge each child to gather leaves that resemble his own leaf.

maple

poplar

oak

Leaves

Leaves That Measure Up

Set up this handy center to reinforce the concept of size. Collect a basketful of fresh fall leaves of varied sizes. Then trace your hand twice at the top of a large sheet of paper. Glue a leaf onto each hand outline—one leaf that is smaller than the hand, and one that is larger than the hand. Sort a few more leaves by this criteria and glue each one to the paper on the corresponding side. Place the paper in your math center, along with the basket of leaves, glue, crayons, and large sheets of paper.

To use the center, a student traces his hand twice on paper. He measures some leaves against his own hand to determine whether the leaves are larger or smaller than his hand; then he glues the leaves in place to create a leaf project similar to the display.

Float 'n' Sort

An "as-sort-ment" of fall fun awaits your youngsters with this water table activity. To prepare, cut a variety of leaf shapes and sizes from autumn colors of craft foam. Place the foam leaves in the water table along with a few Styrofoam® meat trays. Encourage children to sort the floating leaves by color, shape, or size onto the meat trays. Then have them dump the leaves back into the water for more sorting fun.

Colors of Autumn

Give your youngsters a preview of the colors of autumn with this paint-and-press project. Collect large, supple, green leaves during the last days of summer. Then discuss what will soon happen to green leaves as fall weather approaches. Stock the art center with white construction paper, fat paintbrushes, and autumn colors of paint, such as brown, orange, and yellow. Instruct each student to paint the vein side of a leaf, then press the painted leaf onto a sheet of white paper. Have her carefully lift the leaf to reveal a colorful leaf print. Encourage her to repeat the process using a variety of colors and overlapping the prints. Your little ones will leave this center with a colorful image of what lies ahead.

Tasty Leaves

Your little ones won't "be-leaf" their ears when you invite them to eat leaves at this teacher-directed center. Purchase a bag of mixed salad greens; then pour the greens into a large clear bowl. Explain to a small group of youngsters that—although they should never pluck a leaf from a houseplant or nibble on a tree leaf in the yard—the leaves of many plants *are* edible. Pass the bowl around for little ones to observe the edible leaves. Give each child a leaf to touch and hold. As the children examine the leaves, record their comments about the looks, smell, and feel of their leaves on a large leaf cutout. Then give each child a few salad greens on a paper plate. (If desired, provide salad dressing for dipping.) As little ones gobble their greens, add their comments about the taste of the leaves to your leaf cutout. Yummy!

Leaves are green. Luke
They smell fresh. Katie
They're soft. Danielle
Some of them are crunchy.
Alex

Leaf Match

Are your youngsters game for a little leaf viewing? To prepare this leaf-matching game, duplicate the desired number of leaf gameboards (page 196) on construction paper. To make different versions of the gameboard, cut the boards so that each one has only nine squares, as shown. Then enlarge one uncut copy of the gameboard and cut apart the 16 squares to serve as game cards. Laminate the gameboards and cards; then place them in a center along with a supply of plastic bingo chips.

At this center, each child in a small group takes a gameboard. One child takes the leaf cards and holds up one card at a time. After carefully viewing the card on display, each player marks the matching leaf on his gameboard with a bingo chip. Continue the game until one player covers all the leaves on her gameboard (or until everyone has covered all her leaves).

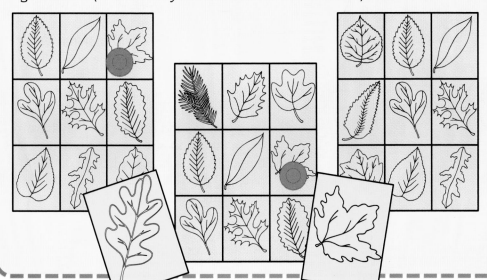

Leaves

Leaves in Action

"Leaf" it to this action rhyme to help little ones learn about opposites. To prepare, use the leaf patterns on page 197 to cut a class supply of construction-paper leaves. Glue each leaf to a craft stick. Give each child a leaf puppet; then lead the class in motions to accompany this rhyme:

The leaves are high.
The leaves are low.
The leaves are blowing soft and slow.

The leaves are up.
The leaves are down.
The leaves are blowing all around.

The leaves are here.
The leaves are there.
The leaves are blowing *everywhere.*

Would You Eat a Leaf?

yes	no
Maria	J. T.
am	Cherlanda
	Emma

Incredible Edible Leaves

Your youngsters will have a hard time "be-leaf-ing" that some leaves are edible. In advance make a chart titled "Would You Eat a Leaf?" Under the title, make a "Yes" column and a "No" column. Ask each child to respond to the question on the chart by placing a sticky note labeled with his name in the corresponding column. Next show children a head of iceberg lettuce, and ask them if they have eaten lettuce in a salad or on a hamburger. As you peel the lettuce off the head, explain that each layer is actually a leaf. Invite children to change their responses on the chart now that they understand that insects aren't the only ones that lunch on leaves.

Problems With Leaves

Even your littlest learners can add and subtract when they use some leafy manipulatives! To prepare, use the leaf patterns on page 197 to cut a supply of construction-paper leaves. Sketch a bare tree on brown craft paper for a storyboard. Then read aloud the rhyming word problems below, inserting numbers appropriate for your little ones' abilities. Invite youngsters to use the paper leaves and the tree to solve the problems.

Addition Rhyme:
One little leaf is on the tree.
___ leaves are on the ground.
Put them all together now.
How many have you found?

Subtraction Rhyme:
___ autumn leaves were on the tree.
The wind blew ___ away.
Look at the tree and tell me, please,
How many leaves did stay?

"That's My Leaf!"

Watch observation skills branch out as your little ones take a close look at leaves. Encourage each child to bring an autumn leaf from home; have a few extras on hand for children who need them. Invite each child to show his leaf to the class. Next call out a descriptive word such as *red,* and then ask all the children with red leaves to hold their leaves high and announce, "That's my leaf!" Continue to call out other adjectives, such as *speckled, pointed,* or *smooth.*

Summer Leaves, Autumn Leaves

Rake in a science lesson by asking youngsters to sort summer and autumn leaves. If you are able, collect enough green leaves and colorful fall leaves to give each child one leaf. (Or cut green, orange, and red leaves from construction paper.) Divide a sheet of chart paper in half; then label one column "Summer" and the other column "Autumn."

Distribute the leaves. Explain that leaves contain *chlorophyll*—a special chemical that helps the leaf turn sunlight, water, and air into food for the tree. It also makes leaves look green. In summer, the leaves make a lot of food for the tree. But in autumn (when there is less sunlight, drier weather, and cooler air), the chlorophyll goes away and the tree gets ready to rest for the winter. When the chlorophyll goes away, the leaf isn't green anymore. It shows its true colors, such as red and orange. After your explanation, ask each child to look at her leaf and decide if it is a summer leaf or an autumn leaf. Help her attach her leaf to the chart in the appropriate column.

Leaves

Impressive Leaves

This activity will "leaf" youngsters with some impressive fine-motor practice! To begin, gather large, fresh leaves in a variety of shapes. Choose leaves with stems and well-defined veins. Put the leaves in your play-dough area with rolling pins, plastic knives, and play dough in autumn colors. Have each youngster flatten a portion of play dough with a rolling pin. Have him press the vein side of a leaf into his play-dough patty. Encourage him to roll the rolling pin over the leaf. Then ask him to carefully cut around the leaf with a plastic knife. Have the child remove the excess play dough. Then instruct him to lift the leaf by its stem, revealing the leafy impression underneath it.

Fall's Afloat

Youngsters will float into some seasonal sorting fun with this fine-motor activity. Place a collection of autumn leaves, acorns, and pinecones in your water table. Provide pairs of tongs and three Styrofoam® meat trays. Invite youngsters to use the tongs to pick up the autumn items; then have them sort the items onto the trays. To expand this activity, draw a leaf on each tray to represent one of three different sizes—small, medium, and large. Then encourage your little ones to sort the leaves by size. Or label each tray with a different numeral; then have youngsters count the corresponding number of items onto each tray. With this idea, students will enjoy practicing an "as-sort-ment" of skills!

Fall Foliage

"Tree-t" youngsters to some colorful fun with this tearing activity. Gather a class supply of fresh autumn leaves in various colors. (If fresh leaves are unavailable, provide construction-paper scraps in fall colors.) Place the leaves in a center along with a class supply of small paper plates, some brown construction paper, and glue. Invite each child to spread glue on her paper plate. Then have her pick out a few leaves and tear them into small pieces. Instruct the child to glue her leaf pieces onto her plate to create a tree-top. Once her treetop is filled with autumn colors, have her tear a brown construction-paper tree trunk to glue to her tree. These trees will make a lovely, leafy display!

Sticky Leaf Collages

Once your youngsters make contact with this activity, you won't be able to peel them away! In advance gather several fresh, autumn leaves (or cut out construction-paper leaves). Cover both sides of each leaf with clear Con-Tact® covering. Then remove the backing from a large sheet of clear Con-Tact® covering. Use packaging tape to attach the sheet to a table with the sticky side up. Invite each child to make a collage by pressing some leaves onto the sticky sheet. Encourage him to peel the leaves off and rearrange them as he desires, creating unique collages. This is one activity your little ones will really stick to!

Leafy Limbs

Invite youngsters to go out on a limb for this tree-decorating activity. To prepare, gather a fallen tree branch with many limbs. Stand the branch in a large pot of plaster of paris and allow the plaster to harden. Next, trace or draw a quantity of leaf shapes on white construction paper. Put the leaf drawings in a center with a container of diluted glue, paintbrushes, bingo dabbers in fall colors, glitter, hole punchers, scissors, and half-lengths of pipe cleaners.

Each student at this center cuts out a few leaves, then uses the bingo dabbers to decorate them. Then she paints her leaves with the glue and sprinkles glitter onto each one. When her leaves dry, she punches a hole in each one. Next, she threads a length of pipe cleaner through each hole and twists it into a loop. She then hangs her leaves on the limbs of the potted tree branch. What a spiffy, sparkly fall tree!

Leaves

Leaf Toss

If you're aiming to rake in some fun, try this beanbag activity. Have the children sit in a large circle around a small clean trash can. Scatter a class supply of beanbags inside the circle. Ask the children to pretend the beanbags are leaves that need to be raked up and placed in the trash. Then ask a few children at a time to each find a leaf. Direct each child to toss his leaf into the trash can from where he found it. Allow each child to have repeated turns tossing the beanbag until he is successful. As a challenge, scatter the beanbags farther away from the trash can but still within the circle.

Whee, Leaves!

Fall into a pile of fun with this parachute activity. In advance gather a parachute, a large rake, and several children's rakes. On a fall day, take your youngsters outdoors to rake a pile of dry leaves. Spread the parachute on the ground; then rake the leaves into the center of the parachute. Have the class gather around the parachute. Ask each child to hold the edge with two hands. Encourage the children to cooperatively lift the parachute up in the air, then lower it gently. Watch the leaves flutter. Next have them use rapid arm movements to flap the parachute to make the leaves take flight. Your youngsters won't "be-leaf" their eyes!

Leaves in the Wind

Here's a leafy activity that is newsworthy. For each child, make one newspaper leaf by cutting a three-foot-long leaf shape from a two-page spread of a newspaper. Give a leaf to each child; then head for the great outdoors. Instruct your youngsters to hold their leaves against their chests. Tell the students to run, letting go of their leaves as they gain speed. Your little ones will be amazed to discover that when they run fast, the leaves stick to their trunks! Look! No hands!

Squirrel Scamper

Feeling a little squirrelly? Then try this nutty balancing act. Explain that in autumn, squirrels balance on tree limbs looking for nuts. Use chalk to draw a long, thin tree limb onto a sidewalk. Then challenge youngsters to balance like squirrels by walking with one foot in front of the other on the limb. Stand at the end of the limb and offer each child a peanut M&M's® candy as a nutty reward for his squirrely behavior.

Puppet Play

Turn your youngsters into "hand-some" autumn trees with the help of hand puppets. In advance make two puppets for each child, one for each hand. To make one hand puppet, cut a five-inch-wide leaf shape from red, orange, or yellow construction paper. Tape together the ends of a 7" x 2" strip of construction paper; then tape the resulting loop to the back of the leaf. During a group time, give two hand puppets to each child. Have her slide four fingers into each puppet's loop. Instruct the children to stretch their arms upward; then invite them to use their hand puppets to dramatize the following action rhyme:

Autumn Leaves
(sung to the tune of "London Bridge")

Leaves are falling to the ground,
Yellow, red, green, and brown.
Leaves are falling from the tree,
Swirling all around me.

Leaves

Fall "Tree-t"

Ingredients:
1 rice cake per child
1/4 carrot per child
peanut butter
Betty Crocker® Decor Selects sugar crystals in green,
    red, and yellow

Utensils and Supplies:
1 plastic knife (or craft stick) per child
napkins
vegetable peeler
knife

Teacher Preparation:
  Peel the necessary number of carrots; then cut off
the pointed tips. Cut each carrot in half; then slice
each piece in half lengthwise. Arrange the ingredients
and utensils near the step-by-step direction cards.

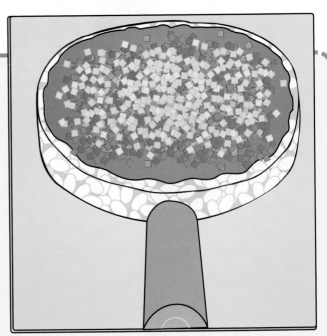

What to Do When the Snack Is Through

  Help size up your youngsters' math skills with the
help of any extra carrots. Cut each leftover carrot into
several carrot sticks of varied lengths; then put all the
sticks in a resealable plastic bag. Prepare a desired
number of plastic bags in the same manner; then put
the bags in a center. Invite little ones who visit the center to put the carrot sticks from a bag in order by size.

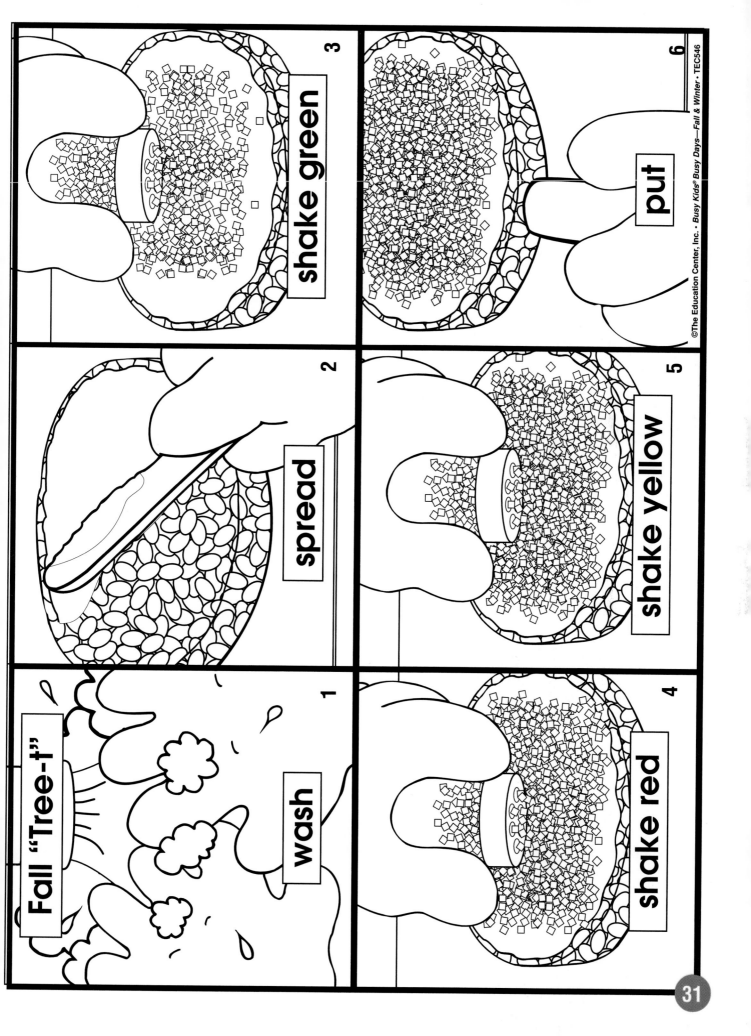

Fall "Tree-t"

wash **1**

spread **2**

shake green **3**

shake red **4**

shake yellow **5**

put **6**

©The Education Center, Inc. • Busy Kids® Busy Days—Fall & Winter • TEC546

Leaves

The Leaves Are Turning

Turn on the excitement as you sing this colorful song about the changing leaves. Gather red, yellow, orange, and brown leaves from outdoors. (Or cut leaf shapes from construction paper.) Then distribute a leaf to each child. As the class sings about each leaf color, have the students with that color stand and wave their leaves in the air.

(sung to the tune of "The Wheels on the Bus")

The leaves are turning strawberry red,
Strawberry red, strawberry red.
The leaves are turning strawberry red,
All autumn long.

The leaves are turning sunshine yellow…
The leaves are turning pumpkin orange…
The leaves are turning mud puddle brown…

Rake 'em Up!

Rake in some reading skills with this song idea. To prepare, write the song on a sheet of chart paper. Then cut out a supply of red, orange, and yellow construction paper leaves. Give each child a few leaf cutouts; then seat youngsters in a circle. Invite them to toss their leaves into the center of the circle. Then appoint a few children to rake the leaves into a pile with toy rakes while the class sings this song. Use a rake handle to point to each word as youngsters sing.

(sung to the tune of "Let's Go Fly a Kite")

Let's go rake the leaves
That fell down from the trees.
Let's go rake the leaves
And make big piles.
Red, orange, and yellow, too.
They're such a sight to view!
Oh, let's all go rake leaves!

Leaves, Leaves, Leaves

This tune is so catchy that it's sure to "leaf" youngsters asking for more!

(sung to the tune of "A Sailor Went to Sea, Sea, Sea")

In fall the trees have leaves, leaves, leaves,
Big rainbow-colored leaves, leaves, leaves.
Red, orange, and yellow leaves, leaves, leaves
That fall down from the trees, trees, trees.

Five Leaves Tumbling Down

Five little leaves
Left on a tree.
The first one said,
"I'd like to be free."

Hold up five fingers.

Hold up one finger.

The second one said,
"There's a breeze in the air."

Hold up two fingers.

The third one said,
"Wiggle, if you dare!"

Hold up three fingers.

The fourth one said,
"Let's float around."

Hold up four fingers.

The fifth one said,
"We're gonna turn brown!"

Hold up five fingers.

Then "Oooh" went the wind,
Blowing round and round.
And the five little leaves
Came tumbling down.

Move hands from side to side.
Circle hands over head.

Wiggle fingers downward.

   As an alternative, select five children to role-play the leaves. Then appoint another child to pantomime the wind. Encourage the class to recite the rhyme, reserving the quotations for the designated leaf or the wind. In the last verse, encourage the wind to dance around while the leaves sway to the floor.

33

Leaves

Oakley's Storytime

Take on the role of Oakley the mighty oak tree when you share books about leaves with your little leaf lovers. Introduce yourself (in your deepest voice) as an oak tree who loves to read books to children about your favorite topic—leaves! Pretend to be Oakley each time you share one of the stories in this unit. To create a treelike appearance, hot-glue real or silk leaves to an old pair of gloves to wear on your hands. Make a leaf hat to wear by hot-gluing leaves to a sentence strip and then stapling the ends of the strip together to fit your head. Your youngsters' enthusiasm over Oakley's storytime will make it worth going out on a limb for!

Red Leaf, Yellow Leaf

Lois Ehlert's *Red Leaf, Yellow Leaf* (Harcourt Brace Jovanovich, Publishers) uses colorful collages to trace the history of a sugar maple tree. After sharing this simple story, return to the first page of the book to examine Ehlert's maple leaf cutout. Flip the page back and forth to see the clever effect. Look for the maple leaf cutout again in the final pages of the book. Then invite your little illustrators to create a leaf cutout that is similar to Ehlert's.

For each child, cut a single maple leaf shape from a sheet of white construction paper. (Vary the placement of the leaf cutout on each child's sheet.) Cover your art table with newspaper; then set it up with autumn-colored paints, paintbrushes, and the cutout sheets. Encourage each artist to paint around the cutout on his sheet as desired. When the paint is dry, have each child tape a sheet of either red or yellow construction paper to the back of his painted paper so that his maple leaf appears to be the color in the background. Display these colorful fall paintings with the title "Red Leaves, Yellow Leaves."

Mitchell

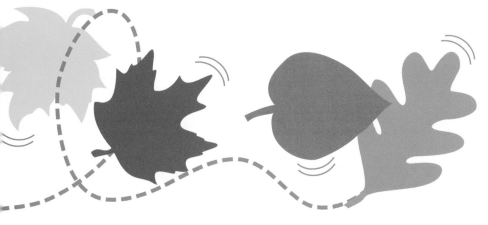

I Eat Leaves

"Unbe-leaf-able" as it may sound, we do eat leaves! JoAnn Vandine's *I Eat Leaves* (Mondo Publishing) explains that—just like many animals—we also eat leaves. Caution your youngsters that they are not to eat just *any* leaf from a plant or tree. Then see if they can name some edible leaves, such as lettuce, cabbage, or turnip greens. After your discussion, teach your little ones this song about leaf eaters.

(sung to the tune of "The Farmer in the Dell")

[Koalas] munch on leaves.
[Koalas] munch on leaves.
While they lunch, they munch and crunch.
[Koalas] munch on leaves.

Create additional verses by substituting these other leaf eaters from Vandine's book for the underlined word: *pandas, caterpillars, rabbits, giraffes, children.*

Fall Is Not Easy

Fall Is Not Easy by Marty Kelley (Zino Press Children's Books) is a humorous look at a tree's many attempts to change its colors with the changing season. After sharing this rhyming text, encourage your little ones to join you at the art table to make silly trees of their own. Set up the center with white construction paper, pencils, several corks, paintbrushes, and tempera paint in different colors. Show the children how to draw a simple tree outline with a pencil or draw the tree shape yourself for younger students. Then encourage children to use their imaginations to decorate their trees in a unique way. Younger children may simply want to dab a cork into the autumn colors and make prints on their trees. Older children may paint their treetops like a rainbow, a smiley face, or a hamburger as Kelley does in his story, or they may create their own unique leaf designs.

Autumn Leaves

Explore shapes and colors with Ken Robbins as he teaches youngsters about 13 different trees and the changes that occur in them during the season of autumn. After reading Robbins' *Autumn Leaves* (Scholastic Inc.), invite the class to search your schoolyard for colorful fall foliage. Try to match the leaves with Robbins's photographs from the book. Then further explore the look of fall leaves with a leaf-making station. To prepare, cover your art table and surrounding floor with newspaper; then place a large bowl of water on the newspaper-covered floor. Die-cut three to five leaves for each child from colorful construction paper. Pour water-thinned paint in fall colors into separate Styrofoam® trays. Clip a piece of sponge to each of several spring-type clothespins; then put a few clothespin paintbrushes in each tray of paint. Have youngsters wear smocks at this station.

To make an autumn leaf, a child uses one hand to crumple a construction paper leaf of his choice; then he opens it and flattens it with his hand. (Younger children may need help with this step.) Using the clothespin paintbrushes, he dabs his leaf with paints in different colors. Next, he swishes his leaf in the bowl of water to blend the colors. Then he places the leaf on newspaper to dry. Use these beautiful, realistic-looking leaves as an autumn bulletin board border or encourage each child to glue his dried leaves to a black construction paper background for a dramatic display.

Fall Harvest

Popcorn Alphabet

Pop into fall with this paper popcorn string that provides practice with alphabet sequencing. In advance, cut 26 popcorn shapes from white construction paper; then label each one with a different letter of the alphabet. Invite youngsters to lay the popcorn pieces in a row on a table or on the floor, in alphabetical order. Depending on your youngsters' skill level, have them use your classroom alphabet display for help.

Pennies at the Patch

Provide practice in counting money by setting up a pumpkin patch in your dramatic-play area. To prepare, collect an assortment of small or miniature pumpkins and gourds. Also gather several baskets, in varying sizes. Attach a card labeled with a money amount from 1¢ to 10¢ to each basket (smaller amounts on the smaller baskets). Put 20 pennies in each of several zippered sandwich bags to serve as money purses. Place the pumpkins, the labeled baskets, and the purses in a center along with a toy cash register.

At this center, one child plays the farmer selling her produce. The other students are shoppers. A shopper chooses a basket, fills it with the pumpkins of his choice, and then pays the farmer the number of pennies indicated on the basket. After all the shoppers have picked and paid, have them replace the pumpkins for the next group of pickers. Then have them help the farmer count out and put 20 pennies back into each purse.

Nuts About Numbers

Set up this nutty center to reinforce numerals and sets. Provide index cards labeled with the numerals 1 to 10 (or other numbers appropriate for your students' ages) and a basket full of unshelled nuts. Each child at this center chooses a numeral card, then counts out a corresponding number of nuts. When he's counted nuts to match each numeral card, check his work and reward his effort by stamping his hand with a squirrel stamp or drawing a simple squirrel on his hand (as shown).

Cash Crop

Cash in on numeral recognition skills by using grocery store ads. For each child in a small group, cut out a fall food and its price from a grocery store advertisement. Glue each ad onto tagboard. Give each child a food card; then ask him to identify the food pictured. Next call out a number from 0 to 9. Have each youngster search his card for the number called. (It might be part of a larger number, such as the 9 in 59.) If he finds the number on his card, he raises his hand and then shows you the number. Continue calling different numbers until all the numbers have been named. Then direct each youngster to switch cards with a classmate before playing another round.

I'm thinking of a food that begins with C.

Harvesting the ABCs

This alphabetical harvest of fruits and vegetables will yield a large crop of letter-sound associations. Collect a variety of real or plastic fruits and vegetables to represent as many beginning sounds as possible. Display the foods in a basket.

Hold up a few of the foods—one at a time—and help youngsters identify the beginning letter for each of your examples. Then play this guessing game with youngsters. To begin, say, "I'm thinking of a food that begins with [letter]." Ask children to guess the food name. If necessary, give additional clues about the food's color, taste, or other characteristics to help students answer correctly. Invite the child with the correct guess to remove that food from the basket. Then, in the same manner, provide clues about another food in the basket. Keep going until your little ones have harvested a crop of letter-sound practice!

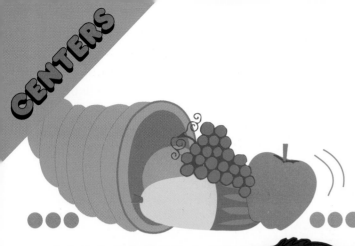

Fall Harvest

Guess the Gourd

Use gourds to strengthen discrimination skills with this small-group activity that can become a center activity. To prepare, gather four gourds in a variety of sizes, shapes, textures, and weights. Invite children to explore each gourd using their senses. Encourage them to discuss how the gourds are alike and different. Then set the four gourds in front of one child. Give him a chance to observe the gourds; then blindfold him. Select one gourd for him to explore with his sense of touch. Then return the gourd to its original place. Remove the blindfold and have the child guess which gourd he was holding. Continue to blindfold other children at the center until all have had a chance to play Guess the Gourd. Once youngsters know how to play this guessing game, invite partners to play it in your discovery center.

"Weigh" to Go!

Here's a "weigh-cool" way to celebrate the fall harvest in your science center. Set up a balance scale next to an assortment of harvest foods, such as apples, small pumpkins, and gourds. Demonstrate how to use the scale if youngsters are unfamiliar with it. Then invite children to visit the center and explore the weights of the various harvest items. As you check in at the center, ask some questions to stimulate comparisons: Which item is heaviest? Which is lightest? Can students make any of the foods balance on the scale? Pound for pound, this center activity carries a lot of weight!

Impressions of Fall

Add fall harvest foods to your play-dough center, and it's sure to make a lasting impression! Gather one or more of the following items: a walnut, an apple, an ear of Indian corn, and a miniature pumpkin. If you choose an apple, cut it in half to reveal the star in the center. Place the food items in a basket at your play-dough center. Provide a few rolling pins. Invite little ones to roll out some play dough, then press or roll each fall food into the dough to make an impression.

Pumpkin Portrait

Give youngsters an opportunity to strengthen fine-motor skills with this pumpkin-painting idea. To begin, spice up a cup of orange paint by adding a teaspoon of pumpkin pie spice to it. Then provide brown paint for the pumpkin stem, as well as some fat paintbrushes. Set an orange pumpkin on a chair by the easel. Then encourage each child to create a fine pumpkin portrait. If desired, display both a large and a small pumpkin; then challenge youngsters to capture the different-sized pumpkins on paper.

Bobbing Berries

Invite youngsters to your water table to try this unique harvesting technique. Explain to youngsters that growers harvest cranberries by flooding their fields and knocking the berries from the vines. The flood waters force the berries to float to the surface of the water so that the workers can collect them. Pour several bags of cranberries into the water table (the berries will float to the top). Provide strainers and a few harvesting scoops created from milk jugs; then have youngsters harvest the floating berries by scooping and depositing them into a strainer to drain. Be prepared for a "berry" good harvest!

Fall Harvest

Pumpkin Patch

Invite your youngsters to join you in the pumpkin patch for this harvesttime fingerplay. Encourage your little ones to use their fingers to represent the five pumpkins, or use orange felt pumpkins on your flannelboard.

Five orange pumpkins growing on a vine,
"Thanks," said the farmer. "This one is fine."
Four orange pumpkins growing on the ground,
A coon ate one without a sound.
Three orange pumpkins under the sky,
"Yum," said the cook. "I'll make pumpkin pie."
Two orange pumpkins lying in the sun,
"Mine," said the baby, and then there was one.
One orange pumpkin left on the vine,
I'll take this one 'cause it's harvesttime!

Apple of My Eye

Polish up critical-thinking skills with this apple game. Purchase a few apples of different colors, sizes, and varieties. Show the apples to the class and ask them to focus on the apples' colors, shapes, and sizes. Then discuss the similarities and differences among the apples. Next, introduce the game. Explain that you are thinking of one apple—the apple of your eye. Give clues to help youngsters determine which apple you've chosen. For example, say "My apple is not red." Guide a student volunteer to remove a red apple from the selection. Continue in this manner until only one apple remains. Then start the apple pickin' all over again!

Fall Picks

Here's a brainstorming activity that is worth pickin'! On chart paper draw a large apple. Invite students to brainstorm different food products that can be made with apples; then chart their responses inside the apple. When your apple list is complete, draw a large pumpkin on another piece of chart paper. Have the children list pumpkin foods and other purposes for pumpkins, such as making jack-o'-lanterns. Then ask each child to select a favorite item from each list. Put a tally mark next to each item each time it is selected. Total the tally marks to determine your class's favorite apple and pumpkin picks.

apple pie   ⫶⫶⫶⫶ ⫶⫶
apple juice   ⫶⫶⫶⫶ ⫶⫶
apple butter   ⫶⫶⫶

Gourd Talk

Reap the benefits of this language activity as your youngsters go goo-goo over gourds! In advance collect gourds of interesting shapes and sizes in a basket. Have your students sit in a circle; then pass around one gourd at a time. Encourage the children to observe the gourds using their senses. Discuss the color, texture, and smell of each gourd. Ask your students to comment on each gourd's shape, size, and weight. As a further challenge, have youngsters determine the similarities and differences between the gourds. Then, during your next circle time, go on to "Groups of Gourds" below.

Groups of Gourds

Extend your exploration of gourds with this sorting game. Use yarn to make one large circle on the floor; then display a variety of gourds around the outside of the circle. Hold up a bumpy gourd and chant the rhyme below. Ask student volunteers to look for the bumpy gourds and place them inside the circle. Brainstorm together other ways to sort the gourds, such as by color, size, or shape. Once you have determined a new characteristic by which to sort, insert the characteristic into the rhyme. Continue grouping by other features in this gourd game of sorts.

Look! Look!
What do you see?
Find other gourds that are [bumpy] like me.

Fall Harvest

Cornhusk Fences

Youngsters will have a "tear-rific" time making these neat cornhusk fences. To prepare, place several ears of corn in a basket. Then put the basket, white construction paper, glue, scissors, and crayons in a center. Invite one small group of children at a time to the center. Encourage the students to take turns tearing the husk from one ear of corn. (You won't need the corn for this activity. Put it aside for printing or cooking later.) Help each child cut some cornhusks into thin strips; then show him how to glue the strips onto a sheet of paper to form a fence. Then have each child draw three orange pumpkins atop his fence. Invite him to glue a copy of the poem shown to his paper. Recite the poem several times as a group; then invite students to take their illustrated poems home to share with their families.

> Three little pumpkins all in a row.
> Sitting on a pretty little fence just so.
> What would happen if the wind should blow?
> Split. Splat. Splatter. Oh no!

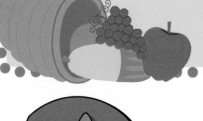

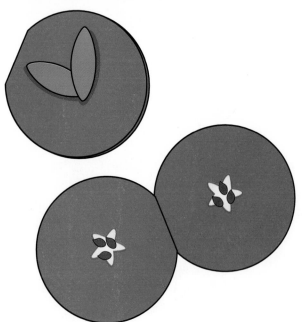

Star-Studded Apples

Invite the apples of your eye to make their own star-studded apples with this idea. For each child, fold a 9" x 12" sheet of red construction paper in half. Draw a circle on the fold. Also for each child, cut two small white stars from construction paper. Place the folded paper, the stars, green construction paper, glue, and scissors in a center.

Before beginning this project, serve apples at snacktime. Cut the apples in half horizontally to reveal the star shape in the center. Ask each child to find the star in her apple half; then have her remove the seeds and place them in a small cup before eating her snack. Next invite small groups to the center you've set up. Invite each child to cut a circle from the red paper, being careful not to cut the fold. Have her cut or tear two leaves from the green paper; then have her glue them to the center of the top circle. Direct her to open her circle cutout and glue a white star to the center of each apple half. As a finishing touch, have her glue her real apple seeds onto the stars to create an apple that "ex-seeds" all others!

Twisted Fall Wreaths

Little fingers will be twistin' and turnin' as your students make these seasonal wreaths. In advance, collect several paper grocery bags. Cut down the side of each bag; then cut off and discard the bag's bottom. Fold the bag flat; then cut it into 3" x 18" strips. Have each child crumple a strip, then twist it into a long cordlike rope. Help him staple the two ends of his paper rope together to make a wreath. Then invite each child to cut three orange pumpkins and three red apples from craft foam or construction paper. Help him staple his cutouts onto his wreath to create a delightful door decoration.

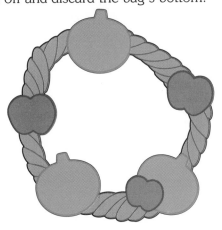

Apple Architecture

Encourage your young architects to pick their best designs for these apple structures. In advance, peel one apple for every two students; then cut each apple into quarters, trimming away the core. Give each child a plastic knife, several toothpicks, and two apple quarters on a paper plate. Invite her to cut her apples into chunks. Then instruct her to insert toothpicks into the apple chunks and build an apple structure. Display this apple architecture in an exhibit that's sure to generate a round of "apple-ause."

Seed Shakers

Shake up a pumpkin exploration with these seed shakers! In advance, ask parents to send in small, clean, plastic bottles with lids. Then bring in a few medium-sized pumpkins. Place the pumpkins on a newspaper-covered table, along with a few cookie sheets, some scoops or large spoons, and permanent markers. Invite one small group at a time to the table; then cut the top off a pumpkin. Ask the children to scoop the seeds out of the pumpkin. Then have them separate the seeds from the pulp and spread the seeds on a cookie sheet to dry. For fun, invite the group members to cooperatively draw a jack-o'-lantern face on the pumpkin.

The next day, set up a center with markers, large adhesive labels, the bottles, and the dried pumpkin seeds. Invite each child at this center to make a seed shaker. Have the child count a designated number of seeds into her bottle. Help her screw the lid securely onto her bottle; then have her write "[Child's name]'s Seed Shaker" on a label. Invite her to decorate her label with markers; then have her peel the label and stick it to her bottle. Ready? Shake it!

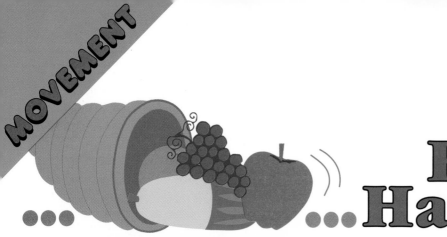

Fall Harvest

Pumpkin Pickin'

Come along for a pumpkin-pickin' hayride! In advance scatter a miniature pumpkin for each child in an outdoor field. For your hay wagon, ask students to stand one behind the other holding onto a rope. Designate one child as the tractor driver; then have him drive ahead of the wagon on a riding toy. Have the children follow your lead as you bounce up and down along the bumpy path to the pumpkin patch. Sing the following song as you bump along:

Here We Go "A-Pumpkining"
(sung to the tune of "Here We Go A-Caroling")

Here we go "a-pumpkining,"
Among the vines and hay.
Here we go a-hunting
For an orange pumpkin today.
Fun and joy come to you,
As you find your pumpkin, too.
May it be the perfect one for a happy harvest treat.
May it be the perfect one for you!

Upon arriving at the pumpkin patch, have youngsters drop the rope; then send them on their way to "pick" pumpkins. Have each child roll his pumpkin back to the rope. With a pumpkin in one hand and the rope in the other, hit the hay for another bumpy ride back.

Happy Harvesting

Put your happy harvesters to work as they reap the rewards of autumn! Gather enough pumpkins, apples, gourds, squash, or corn so that each child will have one fall item. (Drawings or pictures of fall items can be substituted.) Then scatter these fall fruits and vegetables at one end of a field while your students form a line at the opposite end. Put a large basket halfway between your students and the fall items. Explain that at the starting signal, each child should run to collect a fall item and deliver it to the basket. When the minute timer rings, harvesttime is over. Set the timer, give the signal, and have youngsters try to gather all the items before the timer rings. Then scatter the fruits and vegetables again, but this time ask youngsters to hop, skip, or gallop their way to the fruits of their labor.

Can You Be an Apple Tree?

Encourage your students to go out on a limb with this quick-response activity. Divide the class into partners. Designate one child in each pair to be an apple tree and the other an apple picker. Ask each apple picker to stand facing his partner. Give each apple tree two pieces of red or green tissue paper to crumple up into apples; then have him hold an apple in each hand with his arms out at his sides. At the count of three, tell him to drop an apple from one hand. The apple picker must quickly attempt to catch the apple before it hits the ground. Count again; then ask the tree to drop his second apple for the apple picker to catch. Then have the partners switch roles.

Squirrel Search

Have your students gone squirrelly? It's bound to happen as your little ones imitate squirrels in search of their winter food supply. In advance hide enough unshelled peanuts around your classroom so that each child can collect four nuts. Then explain that squirrels gather berries, nuts, and seeds to store as their winter food supply. Divide your class into small groups; then have one group at a time scamper around the room on all fours, searching for hidden nuts. Ask each squirrel to stop once he has found four nuts. After all your little squirrels have finished their searches, pretend that winter has arrived early and have them dig into their food supply!

Popular Popcorn

Of all the corn harvested in the fall, popcorn is perhaps the most popular with children. Bring in some popcorn on the cob. Place one cob in a small brown paper bag, fold the top down, and put it in a microwave oven for approximately two minutes until the corn pops. (If you can't find popcorn on the cob, pop some regular microwave popcorn.) Then ask your little ones to simulate the popping process. Use two long jump ropes to make the shape of one large corncob. Ask each youngster to squat inside the corncob with his head tucked down toward his knees. Then turn on the heat as you sing the song below, and watch your kernels explode with excitement!

Pop Goes the Popcorn
(sung to the tune of "Pop! Goes the Weasel")

All along the popcorn cob,

The kernels get all heated.
They get so hot, they want to pop.
POP! Goes the popcorn!

*Squat with head
   tucked toward knees.
Shake body slowly.
Shake body quickly.
Jump up and down.*

45

Fall Harvest

Potato Pal

Ingredients:
1 baked potato per child
string beans
broccoli flowerets
baby carrots
raisins
red peppers
butter (optional)

Utensils and Supplies:
1 paper plate per child
plastic forks
knife

Teacher Preparation:

Bake one potato for each child; then cool. Wash all of the vegetables. Separate the broccoli flowerets, slice the peppers, and cut the carrots in half. Arrange the ingredients and utensils near the step-by-step direction cards. If desired, have butter available for children who wish to add it to their baked potatoes when it is time to eat the snack.

What to Do When the Snack Is Through

Harvest some fall fun with this printing project. Draw a large cornucopia shape on bulletin-board paper. Lay it on the art table next to the following supplies: several shallow containers of tempera paints in autumn colors, raw potato halves, and other vegetables left over from the recipe. Invite your children to dip the various vegetables into the paints and then make prints of the vegetables directly on the cornucopia. When the paint is dry, display this collaborative cornucopia for all to see!

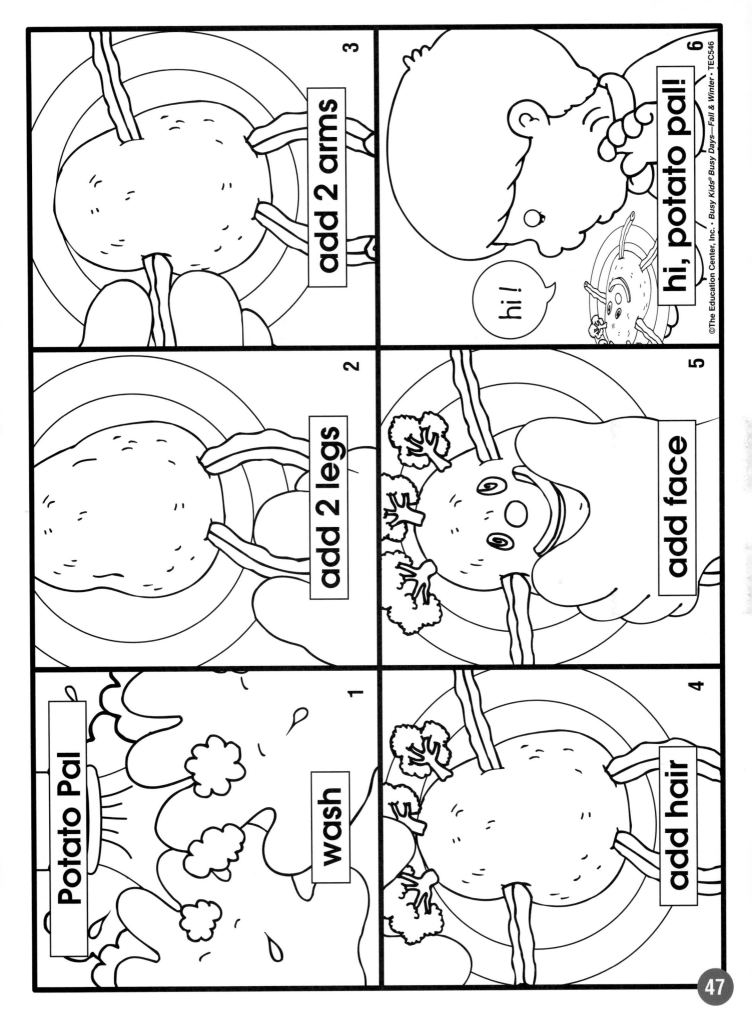

©The Education Center, Inc. • Busy Kids® Busy Days—Fall & Winter • TEC546

Fall Harvest

In the Farmer's Hands

(sung to the tune of "He's Got the Whole World in His Hands")

The farmer's got [pumpkins] in his hands.
The farmer's got [pumpkins] in his hands.
The farmer's got [pumpkins] in his hands.
'Cause harvesttime is here again.

Substitute *apples, green beans,* or *carrots* for the underlined word each time you repeat the song. Or encourage youngsters to think of their own foods to add to the song.

Bountiful Basket

Little ones will build a bountiful vocabulary of fall harvest foods with this song. To prepare, gather a basket and the food items named in the song. Distribute the foods to students; then sing the song. As each item is named, have the youngster holding that food place it in the basket. Repeat the song until every child has had a turn to place a fall food in the basket.

(sung to the tune of "Are You Sleeping?")

It is harvesttime. It is harvesttime.
Time to pick, time to pick.
Pumpkins, apples, green peas,
Corn and squash and berries.
Harvesttime. Harvesttime.

After learning the song, encourage your little farmhands to cut out construction paper pumpkins, apples, peas, corn, squash, and berries. Display all these yummy fall foods with a large construction paper basket to create a bountiful bulletin board.

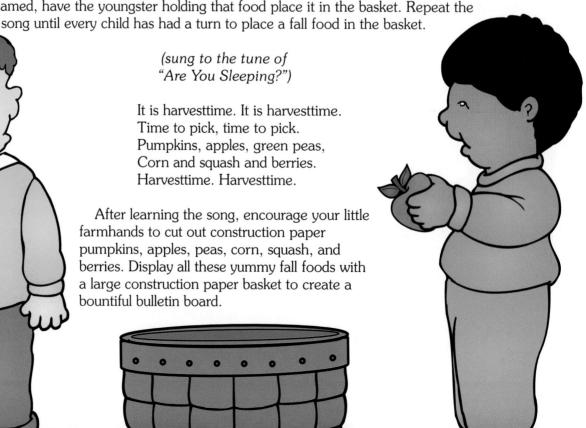

Foods to Harvest

(sung to the tune of "There's a Hole in the Bucket")

There are pumpkins to harvest,
To harvest, to harvest.
There are pumpkins to harvest
From the garden's vines.

There are corn ears to harvest,
To harvest, to harvest.
There are corn ears to harvest
From the garden's stalks.

There are apples to harvest,
To harvest, to harvest.
There are apples to harvest
From the orchard's trees.

Thank You, Mr. Farmer!

(sung to the tune of "I'm Popeye the Sailor Man")

Oh, farmer at harvesttime,
You work in the bright sunshine.
You always do your best
To have a good harvest,
We thank you at harvesttime!

49

Fall Harvest

Apples and Pumpkins

Enjoy a trip to the farm for some apple and pumpkin pickin' as you read *Apples and Pumpkins* by Anne Rockwell (Aladdin Paperbacks). As a follow-up, invite your youngsters to do some fall harvest estimating. Cut out a class supply of red construction paper apples. Fill a bushel basket (or smaller basket) with real apples. Ask youngsters to guess how many apples are in the basket; then ask each child to record her name and estimation on a construction paper apple. Count the apples together to determine the actual number. Discuss the estimates. Whose was closest? Which were too high? Too low? Then munch and crunch those yummy apples for a snack or use them to make applesauce.

For an "a-peel-ing" bulletin board, tack the empty bushel basket (on its side) to the board and add the paper apples with the children's estimates so that they appear to be spilling out of the basket. Add the poem shown to finish the display.

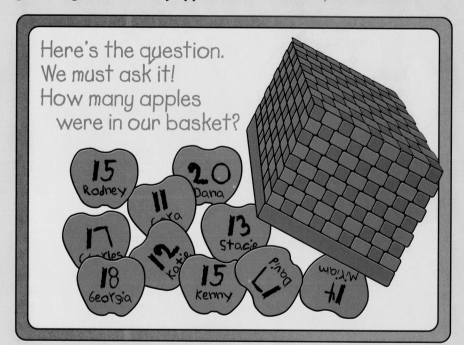

Here's the question. We must ask it! How many apples were in our basket?

15 Rodney
20 Dana
11 Raya
17 Charles
12 Katie
13 Stacie
18 Georgia
15 Kenny
17 David
14 Miriam

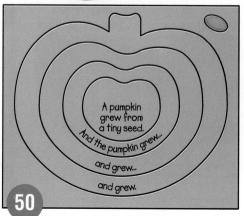

A pumpkin grew from a tiny seed.
And the pumpkin grew...
and grew...
and grew.

Pumpkin Pumpkin

You're sure to see youngsters' enthusiasm grow as they watch Jamie's pumpkin grow...and grow...and grow in Jeanne Titherington's *Pumpkin Pumpkin* (Mulberry Books). After sharing this classic, invite your little ones to make pumpkin puzzles. Draw a pumpkin shape (as shown) on orange paper. Program the graduated "rings" on the pumpkin design as shown. Photocopy a class supply of the programmed drawing on orange construction paper. Next, gather a class supply of pumpkin seeds and place them at a classroom center, along with the pumpkin patterns, scissors, and glue.

To make a pumpkin puzzle, the child cuts out the largest pumpkin. Then he folds the cutout in half—with the lines showing on the outside—and cuts out each smaller pumpkin. (Give help as needed.) Once all four pumpkins are cut out, he glues a pumpkin seed to the smallest pumpkin. Show him how to put his pumpkin puzzle together by sequencing the pumpkins from smallest to largest. Help him read aloud the writing on the pumpkin as he assembles it. Store the pumpkin puzzles in resealable plastic bags and encourage children to share them with their families.

Too Many Pumpkins

What's Rebecca Estelle to do when she finds herself surrounded by an entire yard full of pumpkins? Get baking, of course! Read aloud *Too Many Pumpkins* by Linda White (Holiday House, Inc.), then serve up a science lesson as you invite youngsters to observe the differences in raw and cooked pumpkin. Show youngsters a small cooking pumpkin (often called a sugar pumpkin). Have them watch as you use a sharp knife to cut the pumpkin in half crosswise. Cut a small chunk off one half and pass it around for children to examine. Talk about the pumpkin's smell, color, and texture. Then place the pumpkin in a baking pan—cut sides down—and ask an adult helper to bake the pumpkin at 325° for 45 minutes or until tender when pierced with a fork. After it cools, return it to your classroom and have youngsters examine how it has changed. Ask student volunteers to help you remove the peel and seeds. Then have everyone take turns using a potato masher to mash the pumpkin.

If desired, use the mashed pumpkin in place of canned pumpkin in your favorite recipe and bake up a class treat of muffins, bread, or pie. Rebecca Estelle would be proud!

Possum's Harvest Moon

Celebrate along with Possum and his friends as they party under the harvest moon in *Possum's Harvest Moon* by Anne Hunter (Houghton Mifflin Company). To create a harvest moon in your classroom, put a circle-shaped yellow transparency on the overhead projector and shine it on the ceiling to resemble the moon. Or invite small groups of youngsters to help paint a large circle from bulletin board paper yellow and then sprinkle the wet paint with gold glitter. Hang the finished moon from the ceiling. Once your harvest moon is in place, invite little ones to sing and dance to this moonlight jig.

(sung to the tune of "This Old Man")

The harvest moon
Rose in the sky,
So Possum said, "Let's jump
   and jive.
Come to my Harvest Moon
   Soiree!
We'll sing and dance till the
   break of day!"

Grandma's Smile

Join a young girl and her grandmother as they enjoy the excitement of an autumn fair in *Grandma's Smile* by Elaine Moore (Lothrop, Lee & Shepard Books). What better way to culminate your fall harvest unit than to have your own class fair? Set up these activities that resemble those in the story.

- Ask parent volunteers to send in doughnuts and apple cider for a fall treat.
- Set up pumpkin relays where youngsters roll pumpkins to a designated spot.
- Together rake some leaves into a pile; then jump in them. Or purchase some hay bales and allow little ones to climb on and jump off them.
- Play some festive music and do-si-do like the girl and her grandmother did in the story.
- Set up a few large pumpkins and invite each youngster to use erasable markers to add a jack-o'-lantern face or a face that reminds him of his grandma's smile.

Spiders and Bats

Active Arachnids

Teach youngsters this song about active arachnids to reinforce number skills. Appoint children to take the roles of Mother Spider and each of the five little spiders. Send the five spiders to a designated "web." During the song, signal the appropriate number of spiders to crawl back to Mother at the end of each verse. Pause to encourage students to count the returning spiders. Repeat the song until every child has had a chance to role-play a spider.

(sung to the tune of "Five Little Ducks Went Out to Play")

Five black spiders went out to play
On a web so far away.
Mother Spider said, "Come back. Come back."
Four little spiders came crawling back.

Four little spiders…
Three little spiders…
Two little spiders…

One little spider went out to play
On a web so far away.
Mother Spider said, "Come back. Come back."
No little spiders came crawling back.

Now Mother Spider was very wise.
She made a meal of tasty flies.
Mother Spider called, "It's time to eat!"
Five little spiders came home for a treat!

Creepy-Crawly Calendar

If it's October, then it's time to update your calendar with these student-made numeral cards. To prepare, give each child a white construction paper square that is sized to fit a numeral box on your class calendar. Invite him to illustrate his square with a spider or bat. Then help him label his card with a designated numeral from the calendar. Replace your ordinary calendar numerals with these spooky bat and spider cards and use them during your daily calendar activities. To reinforce numeral recognition skills, occasionally ask a child to identify his calendar card and the numeral on it.

Batty Shapes

Use this idea to bat around the notion that bats might be found in many different sizes and shapes. To prepare, give each child a sheet of white paper and a black crayon. On your own paper, show youngsters how to draw a bat using a variety of sizes of a single shape. For example, you might draw an oval bat body with two oval wings and small oval eyes. Then challenge youngsters to draw their own bats using shapes such as diamonds, triangles, rectangles, circles, squares, or hearts. Invite each little one to share his drawing with the class; then ask the class to identify the shape used for the bat.

The Bats Are Out Tonight

Set youngsters' sights on counting skills with this nocturnal number song. If desired, cut out ten felt bats for flannelboard use with the song. Or encourage youngsters to hold up the appropriate number of fingers as they sing along.

(sung to the tune of "When the Saints Go Marching In")

Oh, when the bats come out tonight,
Oh, when the bats come out tonight,
Oh, I will count them as they fly by,
When the bats come out tonight.

Oh, I see one, two, three, four, five,
Oh, I see six, seven, eight, nine, ten.
Oh, how I love to count those night creatures,
When the bats come out at night.

Repeat the first verse.

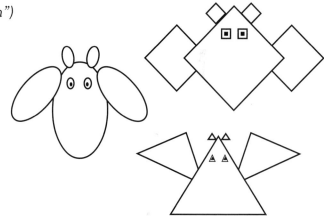

Bat Match

Youngsters' number skills will take flight with this batty activity. Enlarge the bat pattern on page 198; then trace and cut out a desired number of black tagboard bats. Use a white paint pen or correction pen to write a different numeral on the right wing of each bat. Affix the corresponding number of Halloween stickers on each left wing. Cut each bat apart at its wings; then place all the pieces in a center. To use, a child assembles each bat by matching a wing set. To vary this activity, program each set of wings with matching uppercase and lowercase letters or with pictures and corresponding initial consonant sounds. For younger students, program each wing pair with identical letters, numerals, or sticker quantities.

Spiders and Bats

I think this is a marble!

Bat Sense

If you look at a picture of a bat, you'll notice that its ears are large compared to the size of its body. Large ears help the bat hear better. Bats use their unique sense of hearing to help them navigate and find food. Invite your youngsters to test *their* sense of hearing with this sensory activity. Collect eight black film canisters; then sort the canisters into pairs. Fill each canister in a pair with an identical item, such as a cotton ball, a penny, a paper clip, or a marble. (Be certain the four pairs of canisters each have different contents.) Fasten the lids onto the canisters; then place them in your discovery center. Also add to the center an envelope containing a sample of the four different items in the canisters.

Invite children who visit this center to use their sense of hearing to do some sound matching. Have them shake the canisters and try to match the pairs by sound. To extend the activity, ask students to place each item from the envelope with the corresponding canister pair. Then have them remove the canister lids to confirm their guesses.

Blind As a...Spider?

Well, actually, most spiders aren't blind. But web-weaving spiders do have poor eyesight; yet they can weave beautiful and intricate webs! Have your little ones imitate spiders' web-weaving abilities with this fine-motor center. To prepare, purchase some six-inch black paper plates. Use a hole puncher to make holes around the perimeter of each plate. Thread a length of white yarn through one of the holes in each plate; then tie the end in place. Wrap tape around the loose ends of the yarn lengths (for ease in lacing). Place the prepared plates in your fine-motor center.

Encourage each youngster at this center to pick up a plate, close his eyes, and attempt to weave a web by "sewing" the yarn in and out of the holes in the plate. (If desired, provide blindfolds for youngsters to wear as they weave.) When he comes to the end of his yarn, have him open his eyes and take a look at his web design.

Eight Legs and Counting

These creepy-crawly spiders will help your youngsters get a leg up on counting skills. To prepare, make a desired number of spider bodies by hot-gluing together large- and medium-sized black pom-poms as shown. Glue two wiggle eyes onto the smaller pom-pom on each spider. For each spider body, cut four black pipe cleaners in half to make eight spider legs. Then place the spider bodies and legs in your math center. Invite each child who visits this center to add eight legs to each spider's body. Watch out, Miss Muffet!

Bat Cave

Set up a bat cave in your reading center to encourage learning about the habits and characteristics of bats. To create a cave, drape a large blanket over a low table. Equip the bat cave with flashlights and an assortment of bat picture books. If desired, make a tape recording of yourself reading facts about bats, and invite youngsters to listen to the tape as they browse through the bat books in the deep, dark cave.

Sand Spiders

Little ones will get all caught up in this spider-filled sand table! Bury an assortment of plastic or rubber spiders, plastic spider rings, and spider-shaped confetti in your sand table. Use black yarn to weave a spider's web around the entire sand table. Be sure to leave large gaps in the web so youngsters can reach through it to play in the sand. Then invite youngsters to sift or dig for spiders in the sand. After they capture a few spiders, help them attach the spiders to the web around the table. This is one webbed site youngsters will want to visit frequently!

Spiders and Bats

Blind As a Bat

"Bat-tle" the misconception that bats are blind. In fact, all species of bats can see almost as well as humans. Explain to your children that bats rely on their senses of sight and smell to help them find food at night. Then challenge your little ones to find food as bats do. Darken the room and set out a tray of fragrant snacks, such as fresh orange slices or peanut-butter crackers. Place the tray at a distance from your students. Can your youngsters see or trace the smell of food in the semidarkness? Once the children have identified where and what the food is, invite them to relax and snack like bats!

Spider Diet

Help your little ones learn about a spider's diet with this silly song that will have a web spinning and children grinning! To begin, discuss with youngsters the types of foods that spiders like to eat, such as grasshoppers, bees, and ants. Then ask them to pretend that they are spiders, spinning a web to catch a tasty meal. What would *they* like to catch for lunch? Begin the web spinning by passing a ball of yarn around a circle of seated youngsters. Have each child hold on to the free section of the yarn with one hand and pass the ball with the other hand. Sing the song below, inviting the child holding the ball of yarn at the end of the verse to name a sensible or silly spider food. Continue spinning the web until everyone has had a turn to name a spider food.

I'm a Hungry Spider
(sung to the tune of "The Itsy Bitsy Spider")

I am a hungry spider, ready for my lunch.
I'll spin a web and catch something to munch!
I'll catch a beetle or a bumblebee.
But what would you catch in your web if you were me?

Leggy Spiders

Get a leg up on your spider unit with this guessing game. In advance gather four pictures—one each of a person, a four-legged animal, an insect, and a spider. Put the pictures in a basket. Show the pictures to the class and discuss the number of legs each creature possesses. Then invite your youngsters to play this guessing game. Ask a student to select a picture from the basket. Say the following chant; then ask the student to count aloud the number of legs belonging to her secret creature. Challenge the other children to determine (from the number of legs) whether the secret creature is man or beast, insect or spider.

2 - 4 - 6 - 8,
Counting legs is really great!
8 - 6 - 4 - 2,
Creature, how many legs have you?

Batty Colors

Little ones will go batty over this colorful fingerplay! In advance prepare a set of five bat finger puppets for each child by cutting two-inch squares from blue, brown, gray, red, and yellow construction paper. Stamp each square with a bat stamp; then tape each square into a cylinder shape sized to fit on a child's fingertip. (Be certain the bat is showing.) Have each child put her finger puppets on one hand. Then sing the following song. As each color of bat is mentioned, have youngsters show their corresponding bat puppets.

Where Is Blue Bat?
(sung to the tune of "Where Is Thumbkin?")

Where is [blue] bat, where is [blue] bat?
Here I am, here I am.
How are you this morning?
Very well, I thank you.
Fly away, fly away.

Where is brown bat…
Where is gray bat…
Where is red bat…
Where is yellow bat…

Hang In There

Teach your little ones about a bat's nighttime flights and daytime sights with this song.

I'm a Little Bat
(sung to the tune of "I'm a Little Teapot")

I'm a little bat. I fly at night,

Searching for food that tastes just right.
When the morning comes, I settle down
And sleep all day turned upside down.

Hands held outstretched with thumbs crossed.
Wave fingers as if flying.
Slowly stop waving fingers.
Turn hands upside down.

Spiders and Bats

Woven Webs

Weave some fine-motor practice into this theme with these wonderful webs. For each child plus yourself, cut an eight-inch square of poster board and a 72-inch length of yarn. Dip one end of each yarn length into glue and let it harden overnight.

Working with one small group at a time, show the children how to punch holes (as shown) in the four corners and in the center of each side of a poster-board square. Once everyone has hole-punched his square, help each child thread his yarn into one corner hole and tape the loose end of the yarn to the back of the square. Then demonstrate how to lace the yarn across the square, first creating an X and then a cross, to make the radiating lines of a spider's web. Then show the children how to weave the remaining yarn over and under the lines to create the circles in a web. When the webs are done, invite another group to give web making a spin.

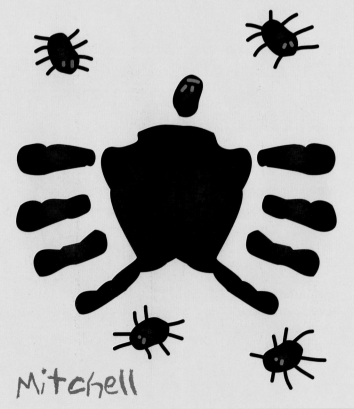

Mitchell

"Hand-some" Spiders

Little ones won't have to look any further than their fingertips to make a handful of spiders. To prepare, put construction paper and several trays of black fingerpaint on a table. Show a small group of youngsters how to make a handprint spider. Holding your thumb up, press the palm and four fingers of one hand into the paint tray. Make a handprint in the middle of a sheet of paper to create a spider body and four legs. Dip your hand in the paint again; then overlap your palm print (holding your hand in the opposite direction) and print the other four legs on the opposite side of your spider. Then make a thumbprint head for your spider. To make baby spiders, simply create thumbprints around the big spider. When the paint dries, draw eight black legs and two red eyes on each thumbprint. What a handsome family of spiders!

Rubber-Band Webs

Your youngsters will stretch their fine-motor skills when they make these rubbery spider webs! Gather a supply of Geoboards and rubber bands. Invite each child in a small group or at a center to stretch rubber bands around the pegs on his board to create a spider-web design. Demonstrate how to stretch bands from corner to corner, top to bottom, or side to side to create the radiating lines of a web. Then have youngsters wrap bands around the pegs on the perimeter of the board to complete the web effect. As a finishing touch, have each youngster add a creepy-crawly plastic spider to his rubber-band web.

Vanishing Bat Act

Invite your little magicians to make these misty bats vanish before their very eyes! In advance, use the bat pattern on page 199 to make a few tagboard tracers. Then fill several spray bottles with water. To make a vanishing bat, have a child place a bat tracer onto a sheet of black construction paper. Invite him to lightly mist the paper with a spray bottle. Then have him remove the tracer from his paper to reveal the image of a bat. Instruct him to keep his eyes on the paper as the wet mist dries and the bat outline vanishes from sight. Once his paper dries completely, invite the child to make a chalk tracing of the bat on his paper. Then encourage him to cut out the bat. Help him attach a length of black yarn to his cutout; then display all the bats from your classroom ceiling.

Goin' Batty

Your youngsters will go batty over these unique fold-and-cut bats. Give each child a 9" x 12" sheet of black construction paper. Then show him how to make a paper bat. To make one, fold the paper in half twice. Hold the paper at the folded corner; then cut a curve across the unfolded corner (as shown). With the paper still folded, cut zigzags along the curve. Unfold the paper; then cut the paper in half along the longer fold to produce a pair of bat wings. For each set of bat wings, fold a black pipe cleaner in half. Slide the wings into the fold of the pipe cleaner; then twist the ends of the pipe cleaner together to create a pair of V-shaped bat ears. If desired, tie a length of black yarn to each pipe cleaner. Then invite your little ones to take their bats outdoors to fly high in the sky.

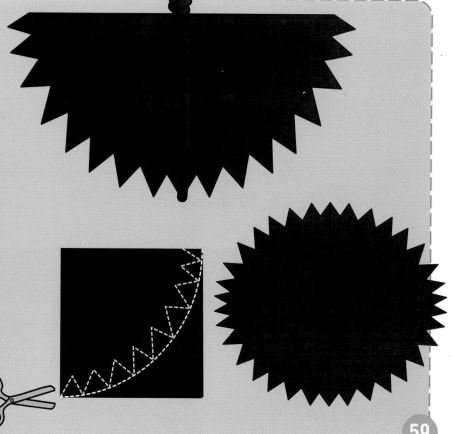

Spiders and Bats

It's a Drag!

Part of being a spider is a drag—or actually, a *dragline*. Spiders spin silk threads called draglines to help them escape from danger. Set up a movement center so your little spiders can experience a dragline first-hand. To prepare, cut a six- to eight-yard length of yarn. Tie one end of the yarn to a heavy piece of furniture near an open area of your classroom. Roll the remaining yarn into a ball and lay it on the floor. When a student visits this center, he pretends to be a spider using his dragline. He takes the ball of yarn and makes his way from the center (his web) to a hiding place in the room. Then he pretends the danger has passed and walks back along the yarn line, tightrope-style. He then winds the yarn into a ball for the next child to use.

Webbed Site

Spin a web of fun around your students as they pretend to be spiders. Thread a long piece of twine or yarn around the chairs, tables, and other furniture in your classroom to make a human-sized spider web. Or create a web outdoors by wrapping twine around playground equipment or branches of trees and bushes. Instruct the children to step over, crawl under, or do whatever it takes to get across this webbed site!

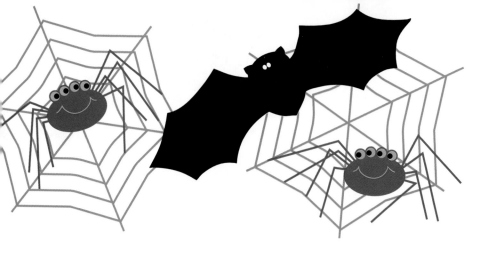

Bug Bites

Provide your hungry little bats with a bug bite! First, divide the class into partners. Designate one child in each pair as the bat. Give each bat's partner a piece of paper to crumple into a loose ball, representing an insect. Explain that real bats fly through the air and catch insects in their mouths, but in this game the bats will catch insects (the paper balls) with their hands. Have each bat's partner toss an insect into the air as the bat attempts to catch it. Once each bat has successfully caught an insect, have the partners switch roles.

Spider Shuffle

Do the Spider Shuffle to highlight that spiders are eight-legged arachnids, not six-legged insects. Divide your class into partners. Count the total number of arms and legs belonging to each pair, emphasizing the number *eight*. Inform students that they are going to become human spiders. First, instruct one partner in each pair to lie down on the floor on his tummy; then have him push himself up onto his extended hands and feet. Next, ask the second partner in each pair to stretch over his partner at a 90-degree angle, touching hands and feet to the floor. Then ask your creepy crawly spiders to attempt to move forward, backward, and sideways. It's the Spider Shuffle!

Daytime/Nighttime

Go batty with this game that demonstrates a bat's backward sleeping schedule. Have your class gather around you. Explain that bats sleep upside down during the day. Bend at the waist (with your head down by your knees) to demonstrate this. Then straighten up and explain that during the night, bats fly around in search of insects to eat. Demonstrate this by holding your arms out at your sides and running around the classroom. Then have your little ones find individual spaces in the room and listen for your commands. When they hear you say "daytime," they should bend at the waist and pretend to go to sleep. When they hear you say "nighttime," they should pretend to fly around in search of food.

Spiders and Bats

Smiling Spider

Ingredients:
1 Oreo® cookie per child
4 five-inch lengths of black string licorice per child
tube of white decorating icing

Utensils and Supplies:
napkins

Teacher Preparation:
   Cut string licorice into five-inch lengths. Gently twist the top and bottom of each cookie to loosen it. Arrange the ingredients and utensils near the step-by-step direction cards.

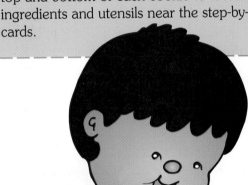

What to Do When the Snack Is Through

   Little ones love to twist open Oreo® cookies to get to the cream filling. And it's a fun way to strengthen fine-motor skills! At another snacktime, give each child two cookies on which to practice his twisting talent. If he breaks a cookie, encourage him to design a cookie creature using the broken pieces and leftover decorating icing. Serve some milk to help wash down these cookie creatures.

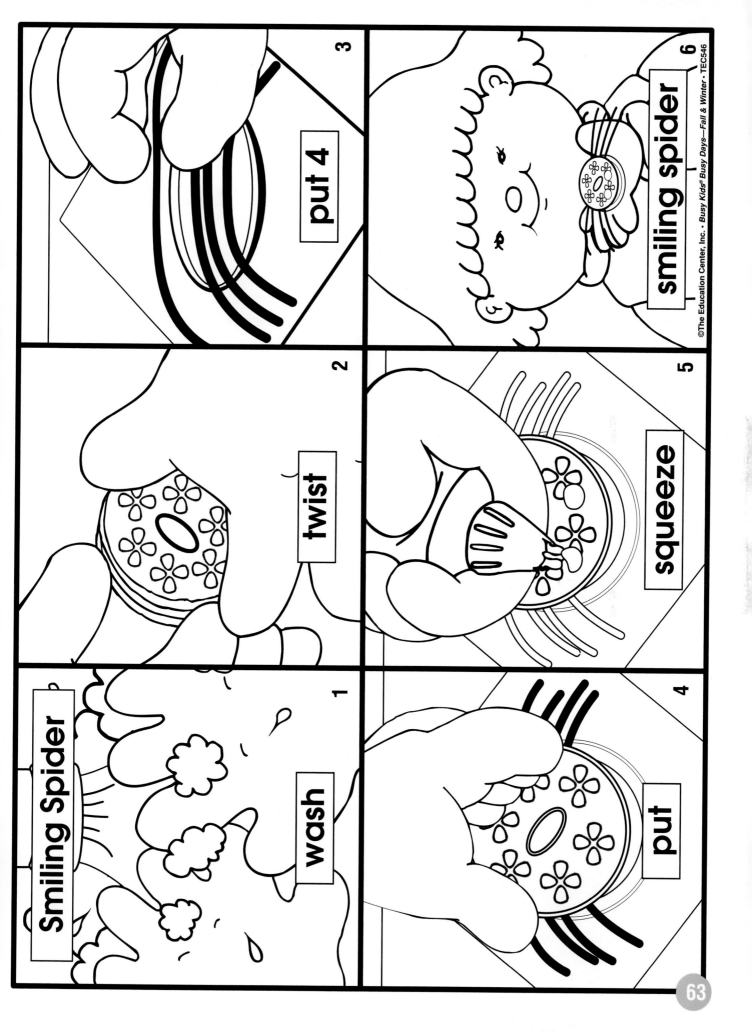

Smiling Spider

wash

1

twist

2

put 4

3

put

4

squeeze

5

smiling spider

6

©The Education Center, Inc. • *Busy Kids® Busy Days—Fall & Winter* • TEC546

Spiders and Bats

Have You Ever Seen a Spider?

Spin some fun into your study of spiders with this song. To begin, seat youngsters in a circle. Give one child a ball of yarn. Instruct him to hold the end of the yarn and then pass the ball to another child. While singing the song, have youngsters pass the yarn from child to child, with each holding a section of the yarn so that a web is created.

(sung to the tune of "Did You Ever See a Lassie?")

Have you ever seen a spider, a spider, a spider?
Have you ever seen a spider spin this way and that?
Spin this way and that way. Spin this way and that way.
Have you ever seen a spider spin this way and that?

The Bats in the Cave

(sung to the tune of "The Wheels on the Bus")

The bats in the cave sleep all day long,
All day long, all day long.
The bats in the cave sleep all day long.
That's what bats do!

The bats in the cave hang upside down,
Upside down, upside down.
The bats in the cave hang upside down.
That's what bats do!

The bats in the cave fly out at night,
Out at night, out at night.
The bats in the cave fly out at night.
That's what bats do!

The bats in the cave catch bugs to eat,
Bugs to eat, bugs to eat.
The bats in the cave catch bugs to eat.
That's what bats do!

Finger Spider

Eight hairy legs,

Lots of eyes,
Two body parts,
There's no disguise
That can hide her—
She's a spider!

*Hold thumbs together. Wiggle
  eight fingers.*
Peek over thumbs.
Wiggle thumbs.
Shake head.
Fold fingers in.
Open fingers and wiggle them.

Spin a Web

*(sung to the tune of
"Row, Row, Row Your Boat")*

Spin, spin, spin a web,
As sturdy as can be.
Spin patiently; then wait and see—
What will your dinner be?

Bat Facts

Teach some friendly bat facts to your class with this rhyme, and maybe your class will agree that bats are nice!

*(chanted to the rhythm of
"Hickory Dickory Dock")*

I think that bats are so nice.
They look like flying mice.
They've got two wings.
They eat flying things.
I think that bats are so nice.

Bats can cause such alarm.
But they never really mean harm.
Their bodies are hairy.
They look a bit scary.
But bats have a lot of sweet charm.

Spiders and Bats

Spider on the Floor

Spin together some hilarious fun as you read *Spider on the Floor* by Bill Russell (Crown Publishers, Inc.). If desired, play Raffi's song "Spider on the Floor" on the album *Singable Songs for the Very Young* (Troubadour Records Ltd.), as you display the pages of the book. Then continue the fun by making spider finger puppets. To make one, glue together two black pom-poms of different sizes for the spider's body. Squeeze glue onto the center of a ¾" x 2" tagboard strip; then drape four 3-inch lengths of black yarn over the glue (as shown). Glue the spider body over the yarn pieces so that there are four yarn legs on each side of the body. When the glue is dry, help the child wrap the tagboard strip around the tip of his index finger; then secure it with tape. During a second reading of the story, invite youngsters to move their finger puppets to the different body parts mentioned in the book.

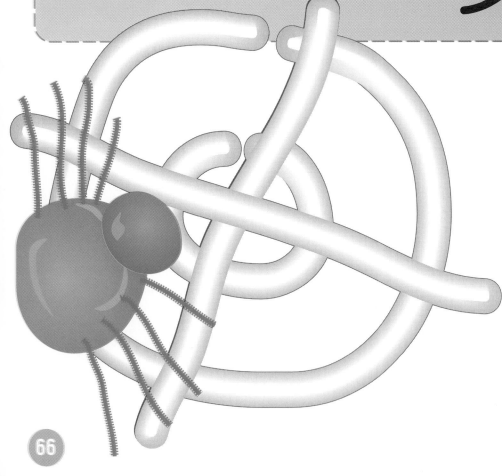

The Very Busy Spider

Get busy reading *The Very Busy Spider* by Eric Carle (The Putnam Publishing Group). Then invite your youngsters to illustrate this popular story using clay. Set up a center with red, green, and white clay (or soft play dough for younger children) and pipe cleaners that have been cut in half. Encourage each student to use her imagination as she works with the clay to form a spider's body and head. Invite her to count eight pipe cleaner halves to use as spider legs. Then show her how to roll thin clay ropes to make a spiderweb. Encourage youngsters to feel the final product just as they can feel Carle's webs in the story.

Stellaluna

Youngsters are sure to go batty over a reading of *Stellaluna* by Janell Cannon (Voyager Picture Books). As a fun follow-up, invite each youngster to make his own Stellaluna. First fold a sheet of brown construction paper in half. Have the child place his thumb on the fold and spread his fingers just a bit. Then trace around his hand. With the paper still folded, have him cut out his handprint and then open it to reveal a one-of-a-kind bat shape. Encourage him to cut bat feet from the paper scraps and glue them to his bat. As a finishing touch, have him stick on two white paper reinforcers for eyes. If desired, hang the bats upside down from a clothesline (or string) in your classroom.

The Itsy Bitsy Spider

Read or sing along to Iza Trapani's extended version of *The Itsy Bitsy Spider* (Whispering Coyote Press, Inc.). After enjoying Trapani's delightful illustrations and additional verses to this ever-popular song, invite your little spider lovers to use watercolors (as Trapani did) to illustrate a page from the story. To prepare, write the verse shown at the bottom of a sheet of white copy paper. Photocopy a class supply; then distribute the papers to your class. Discuss things the children may wish to include in their illustrations, such as a tree, the spider, the sun, and a self-portrait. If desired, make your own watercolor illustration to use as an example.

Encourage little ones to use pencil to draw simple outlines before filling in each outline with watercolors. When the illustrations are complete, display them with the title "The Itsy Bitsy Spider and Me!"

The itsy bitsy spider climbed up the maple tree.
She slipped on some dew and landed next to me.

Bat Jamboree

It will be standing room only during your reading of Kathi Appelt's *Bat Jamboree* (Mulberry Books). As a follow-up to this sassy, rhythmic counting book, have your little bat lovers sing the following song with "bat-itude."

(sung to the tune of "Sing a Song of Sixpence")

At the bat jamboree	Flap like a bat.
The bats put on a show.	
See them build a pyramid	Put thumbs and fingertips together to form triangle.
Standing in ten rows.	Hold up ten fingers.
1, 2, 3, 4, 5, 6,	Count six fingers.
7, 8, 9, 10.	Count remaining fingers.
Until the bat lady sings	Sing, "Laa."
You know the fun won't end!	

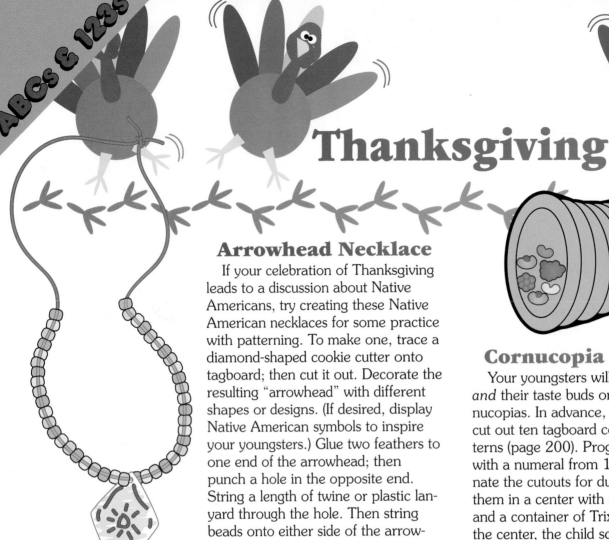

Thanksgiving

Arrowhead Necklace

If your celebration of Thanksgiving leads to a discussion about Native Americans, try creating these Native American necklaces for some practice with patterning. To make one, trace a diamond-shaped cookie cutter onto tagboard; then cut it out. Decorate the resulting "arrowhead" with different shapes or designs. (If desired, display Native American symbols to inspire your youngsters.) Glue two feathers to one end of the arrowhead; then punch a hole in the opposite end. String a length of twine or plastic lanyard through the hole. Then string beads onto either side of the arrowhead, creating a pattern with two or three different colors. Tie the ends of the necklace together; then invite each child to model her special jewelry with pride.

Cornucopia Counting

Your youngsters will feast their *eyes* and their taste buds on these fruity cornucopias. In advance, copy, color, and cut out ten tagboard cornucopia patterns (page 200). Program each cutout with a numeral from 1 to 10; then laminate the cutouts for durability. Place them in a center with napkins, a scoop, and a container of Trix® cereal. To use the center, the child scoops some cereal onto a napkin. Then she counts out and places the appropriate number of cereal pieces onto each cornucopia. Have her check her work for accuracy. Then invite the child to snack on the cereal for a fruity feast!

Dressing the Turkey

This turkey activity is stuffed with all the right ingredients to cook up a batch of letter skills. In advance, cut out one large and one small construction paper turkey body. Then cut out a set of 26 proportionally sized construction paper feathers for each turkey body. Program each large feather with an uppercase letter and each small feather with a lowercase letter; then laminate all the pieces. To use, display the turkey bodies on the floor during group time. Distribute the feathers to students. Then have your class "feather" the turkeys alphabetically, starting on the left side of each turkey. Each time a child places his feather on a turkey, invite him to proudly strut back to his seat. Afterward, put the feathers in a center along with wipe-off markers. Invite each child to trace the letters and then pair the uppercase and lowercase letters. To prepare the center for the next li'l gobbler, simply wipe the feathers clean with a paper towel.

A Shipshape *Mayflower*

It's sure to be smooth sailing when your youngsters make this picture of the *Mayflower* with various shapes. In advance, cut sponges to create semicircles, rectangles, squares, and triangles (refer to the illustration for sizes). Place the sponge shapes in your art center, along with shallow trays of paint in different colors, markers, and sheets of light blue construction paper. Use the sponges to create a sample project to which students may refer.

A child at this center sponge-paints the various shapes (in her choice of colors) onto a sheet of light blue paper to create a picture of the *Mayflower*. She uses a marker to create the lines for the sails and to write her name on her paper. Challenge each artist to identify each shape used in her picture and to count the number of each shape used.

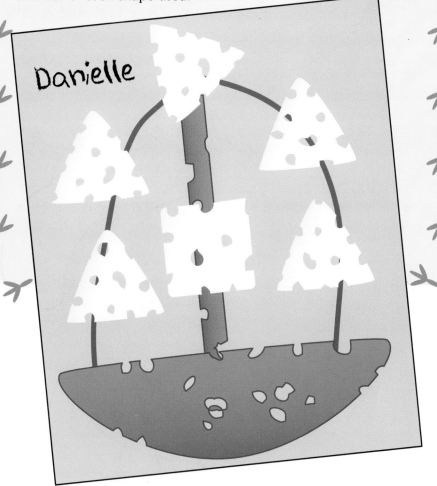

We're Thankful For...

Help youngsters recognize the people, places, and things for which they are thankful this Thanksgiving. In advance, display a large bulletin-board-paper turkey body. Then cut out a set of three large construction paper turkey feathers for each child, plus one set for yourself. Label each of three baskets with "person," "place," or "thing." Then discuss with your students the many things for which they are thankful. Ask each child to illustrate a person for whom she is thankful on one of her feathers. Likewise, have her illustrate a place and a thing on her remaining feathers. (Illustrate your own three feathers in the same way.) Point out the labels on the baskets. Show students each of your feathers; then place each in the corresponding basket. Invite youngsters to sort their feathers in the same way. Then display the feathers, arranging them by category on the turkey. Title the display "We're Gobblin' Grateful for These People, Places, and Things."

Thanksgiving

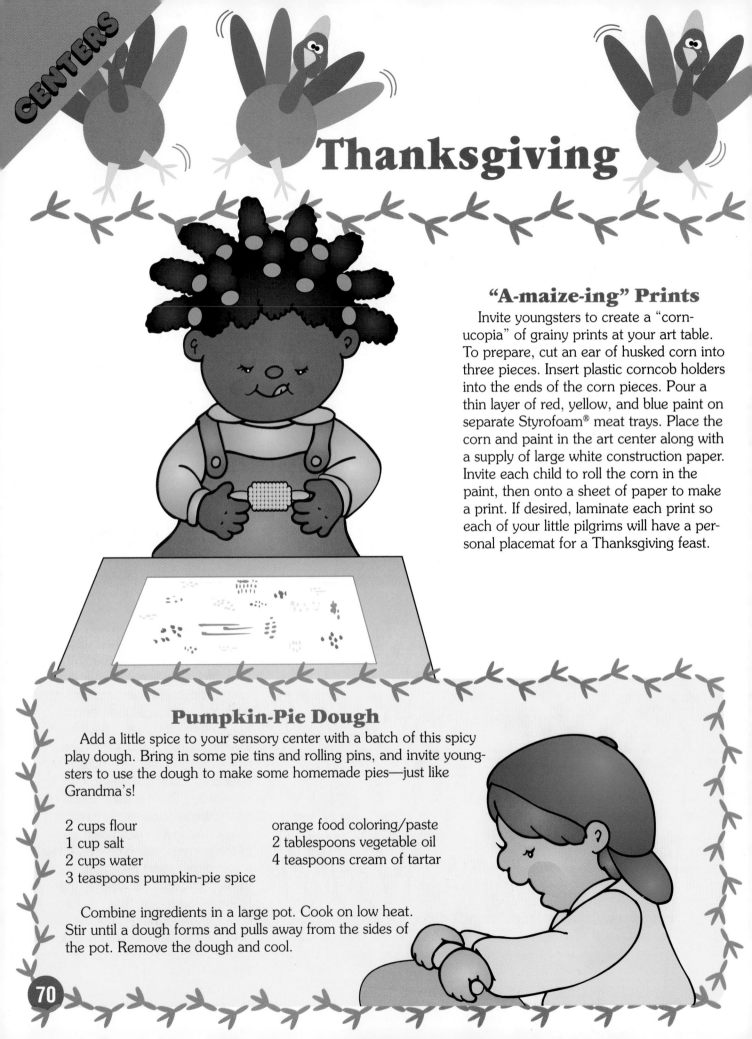

"A-maize-ing" Prints

Invite youngsters to create a "corn-ucopia" of grainy prints at your art table. To prepare, cut an ear of husked corn into three pieces. Insert plastic corncob holders into the ends of the corn pieces. Pour a thin layer of red, yellow, and blue paint on separate Styrofoam® meat trays. Place the corn and paint in the art center along with a supply of large white construction paper. Invite each child to roll the corn in the paint, then onto a sheet of paper to make a print. If desired, laminate each print so each of your little pilgrims will have a personal placemat for a Thanksgiving feast.

Pumpkin-Pie Dough

Add a little spice to your sensory center with a batch of this spicy play dough. Bring in some pie tins and rolling pins, and invite youngsters to use the dough to make some homemade pies—just like Grandma's!

2 cups flour
1 cup salt
2 cups water
3 teaspoons pumpkin-pie spice

orange food coloring/paste
2 tablespoons vegetable oil
4 teaspoons cream of tartar

Combine ingredients in a large pot. Cook on low heat. Stir until a dough forms and pulls away from the sides of the pot. Remove the dough and cool.

Cornmeal to Feel

Invite little ones to the sensory center to get a feel for this cornmeal activity. To prepare, replace the sand in your sand table with cornmeal supplied by parents. Or place a large tub of cornmeal on a low table. Then equip the center with measuring cups, bowls, and spoons. Explain to students that a Wampanoag Indian named Squanto taught the Pilgrims how to plant corn. The Pilgrims used the corn to make corn bread, hoecakes, and Indian pudding. Invite youngsters to the sensory center to explore this grainy food source. After several days of free exploration, move the cornmeal from the sand table to the cooking center. In that center, use a new package of cornmeal to make corn muffins for snacktime. Use the cornmeal from the sensory center to make corn muffins to feed the birds.

Gourds and Potatoes and Pumpkins, Oh My!

Give your discovery center a seasonal twist with some traditional Thanksgiving foods. Display a variety of fresh gourds, regular and miniature ears of Indian corn, walnuts, minipumpkins, sweet potatoes, and squash. Cut open some of the gourds, potatoes, and squash, and crack open a couple of walnuts. Place the cut foods in a shallow tub to contain any possible mess, and keep a container of disposable wipes nearby for quick cleanups. Provide several magnifying glasses; then invite children in this center to examine the items—inside and out—using their senses of sight, touch, and smell.

Nuts!

Your youngsters will go nuts over this addition to your sensory center! Pour a bag of assorted mixed nuts (unshelled) into a large tub. Add tongs, ice-cube trays, and egg cartons. Encourage each child who visits this center to fill an ice-cube tray or egg carton by using the tongs to place a nut in each section of a carton or tray. Children may choose to sort the nuts by type or size as they work. After students enjoy sorting and placing the nuts, add a nutcracker to the center. Your little ones will crack up over this fun method of fine-motor practice!

Thanksgiving

Gobblin' Good

Practice counting as your little turkeys sing this gobblin' good tune. Have youngsters display the corresponding number of fingers while counting forward and backward. For added fun, select ten children to act out the song. Signal each of the ten little turkeys to stand in turn as you sing the first stanza and sit in turn during the second stanza.

Gobble, Gobble
(sung to the tune of "Ten Little Indians")

1, 2, 3, a-gobblin',
4, 5, 6, a-gobblin',
7, 8, 9, a-gobblin',
10 little turkeys gobblin'.

10, 9, 8, a-gobblin',
7, 6, 5, a-gobblin',
4, 3, 2, a-gobblin',
1 little turkey gobblin'.

A Pilgrim's Perspective

As your little ones discuss life as it was during the first Thanksgiving, encourage them to act out the lines and create new verses for this song.

Let's Rock at Plymouth!
(sung to the tune of "We Wish You a Merry Christmas")

The Pilgrims were busy catching fish.
The Pilgrims were busy catching fish.
The Pilgrims were busy catching fish.
Oh, what a day's work!

The Pilgrims were busy planting corn…
The Pilgrims were busy finding berries…
The Pilgrims were busy hunting deer…

The Word Bird

Strengthen vocabulary as your youngsters add a plumage of Thanksgiving words to this featherless fowl. To prepare, cut a feather for each child and one large featherless turkey from construction paper. (Or draw a turkey on your chalkboard.) Each day during the month of November, solicit from a student volunteer a Thanksgiving-related word, such as *turkey, Pilgrims,* or *cranberries.* On a single feather, make a simple drawing to illustrate the word, and label it in large print. Then tape the feather to the turkey. As each new feather is added, have the class review all the previous Thanksgiving words. Challenge older children to read the words as you point to them in random order. For added fun, encourage the children to copy and illustrate the words into a class book about Thanksgiving.

A Basket of Blessings

Your students are certain to learn how much they have to be grateful for as they pass a basket of blessings. Explain to your youngsters that during the Pilgrims' first winter in their new land, they did not have enough food. But by Thanksgiving they were thankful to eat the corn and other crops that they had grown. Then give each child a single kernel of unpopped corn. Pass a small basket around the circle. Have each child name one food for which he is thankful as he puts his kernel in the basket. In the following days, have children put more kernels in the basket as they name other things for which they are grateful concerning school, nature, and their families.

Terrific Turkey Talkin'

Reinforce ordinal numbers with this fingerplay about some frightened fine-feathered friends.

Five little turkeys behind a stack of hay,	
The first one said, "I really hate this day!"	*Put hands over eyes.*
The second one said, "There's a farmer over there!"	*Put hands on hips.*
The third one said, "We don't have a prayer!"	*Point in one direction.*
The fourth one said, "This isn't any fun!"	*Put hands together as if praying.*
The fifth one said, "Let's run and run and run!"	*Make a sad face.*
So they all took a deep breath,	*Pretend to run.*
And off like a shot,	*Take a deep breath.*
The five little turkeys escaped from the pot!	*Make zooming motion with hand.*
	Cheer.

After your little ones have memorized the fingerplay, assign five student volunteers to each play the role of one of the turkeys. Signal each turkey to recite his line; then have the rest of the class say the remaining lines with you.

Thanksgiving

A Flock of Fringed Feathers

These fringed-feather turkeys will provide your youngsters with some gobblin' good fine-motor practice. To prepare, purchase two sturdy six-inch paper plates per child. Then make one copy of the turkey pattern on page 199. Mask the turkey's body on the copy; then enlarge and duplicate the turkey's head and neck until you have a pattern of the desired size. Duplicate a class supply of the pattern on red construction paper. Then cut a supply of construction-paper feathers.

To make a turkey, paint two paper plates brown. While the plates dry, cut out a turkey pattern; then attach a hole-reinforcement eye to each side of the cutout. Fringe several paper feathers by snipping along the sides of each one. Then tape the head cutout and feathers to the rim of one plate. Staple the two plates together along the rims. Send these turkeys home to decorate youngsters' homes for the Thanksgiving holiday.

Our Fine-Feathered Friends

Your little flock can strut its stuff with these fantastic fowl. For each child, duplicate the turkey pattern on page 199 on white construction paper. Prepare several trays of paint in autumn colors. Place a large feather in each paint container. Invite each child in a small group to cut out her turkey. Then have her feather-paint her cutout with the colors of her choice. Once the paint dries, have the child give her turkey a hole-reinforcement eye. Then instruct her to cut several strips of brown paper. Have her glue the strips onto a sheet of construction paper to represent a split-rail fence; then ask the child to glue her turkey to the top of the fence. What a fabulous, feathery flock!

Good-Looking Gobblers

Your little turkeys will have plenty to gobble about when they make these colorful Thanksgiving pictures. Give each child a sheet of tagboard and crayons; then show students how to draw a turkey with a circle body, a half-circle head, dot eyes, a V-shaped beak, a curvy red wattle, and large oval tail feathers. Invite each child to draw and color his own turkey; then have him glue dried beans onto his turkey's feathers for extra flair. These turkeys are gobble-gobble-gorgeous!

Terrific Turkey Tails

Your little turkeys will strut their tail feathers right over to this combination fine-motor and color-matching center. To prepare, make a copy of the turkey pattern on page 199. Mask the feathers; then duplicate the turkey pattern on different tagboard colors. Cut out and laminate each pattern. Put the cutouts and a supply of plastic clothespins (in matching colors) in a center.

Invite each child at this center to clip clothespin "feathers" onto the body of a turkey cutout of the same color. After the child finishes, provide her with a flock of compliments; then have her remove the feathers for the next center visitor. If desired, adapt this activity later by writing a numeral on each turkey. Then invite each child to attach the appropriate number of tail feathers to each turkey.

Cranberry Creations

Cranberries are the fruit of the season, so invite your little Pilgrims to enjoy this "berry" fun drawing activity. In advance freeze a package of fresh cranberries. After sharing books about the first Thanksgiving with your class, discuss the different foods eaten by the Pilgrims and Native Americans during the first Thanksgiving feast. Then take your class outdoors to a sidewalk or concrete area. Draw a large chalk outline of a tabletop on the concrete. Then give each child a frozen cranberry. Invite him to use the fruit to draw a picture of a food from the first Thanksgiving. Use chalk to label each drawing. These cranberry creations look good enough to eat!

Thanksgiving

Turkey for Thanksgiving

Find out who's faster in this ball race—the turkey or the farmer. Have youngsters sit in a circle. Refer to a small ball as the turkey. Ask the students to slowly pass the ball around the circle. After the turkey has been passed around the circle a couple of times, refer to a second ball of another color as the farmer. Start the second ball moving around the circle. Have students increase their passing speeds; then watch them giggle and gobble as the farmer tries to catch the turkey!

Turkey Trot

"Wattle" you know? It's the Turkey Trot! Have your little gobblers form a circle; then give a construction-paper turkey shape to each child. Invite youngsters to trot with their turkeys to this Thanksgiving tune.

Turkey Trot
(sung to the tune of "The Hokey-Pokey")

You put your turkey in.　　　　　　*Hold turkey inside the circle.*
You put your turkey out.　　　　　　*Hold turkey outside the circle.*
You put your turkey in,　　　　　　*Hold turkey inside the circle.*
And you shake it all about.　　　　*Shake the turkey.*
You do the turkey trot,　　　　　　*Strut in place.*
And you turn yourself around.　　　*Turn around in place.*
That's what it's all about.　　　　*Bend knees three times.*

Fun and Games

At the first Thanksgiving, the Pilgrims and Native Americans feasted and played games for three days! They had foot races and jumping contests. Have your little ones list some jumping and running games they would like to play outdoors; then head out to your playground. Youngsters might try seeing who can jump the farthest distance, running a relay race, or seeing how many times they can jump or run around the playground perimeter. As your little ones pretend to be Pilgrims and Native Americans, everyone will have a moving experience!

Let's Talk Turkey

Give your little ones plenty to gobble about as they strut like turkeys. Impersonate a turkey by stretching your neck and tucking in your chin. Tuck your hands under your arms, with elbows at your sides. Scratch the ground with your feet; then walk with a slow, stiff strut. Don't forget to add some turkey talk—"Gobble, gobble!" Invite students to follow in your turkey steps as they strut their stuff to this bird beat:

Turkey Strut
(sung to the tune of
"The Mulberry Bush")

This is how the turkey struts,
   turkey struts, turkey struts.
This is how the turkey struts.
The turkey struts like this.

Dance to the Beat

Invite little ones to dance to the beat—just as the Native Americans probably did at the first Thanksgiving. Your youngsters will enjoy making rattles to accompany their dancing. To make a rattle, a child paints an empty toilet-paper tube bright colors. When the paint is dry, staple one end of his tube shut. Use a funnel to pour dried beans into the open end; then staple it shut as well.

Have youngsters form a circle; then invite them to dance around the circle as they shake their rattles to a drumbeat. If a drum is unavailable, simply chant, "1-2-3-4, 1-2-3-4," placing the emphasis on the fourth beat. Encourage youngsters to hop and stomp their feet with their rattles behind their backs, by their knees, or over their heads. Invite them to create their own dance movements as they shake, rattle, and roll!

Thanksgiving

Gobble! Gobble!

Ingredients:
1 large round cookie per child
1 chocolate Nutter Butter® cookie per child
3 candy corns per child
2 peanut-butter chips per child
tube of red decorating gel
6 pretzel sticks per child

Utensils and Supplies:
napkins

Teacher Preparation:
Arrange the ingredients and utensils near the step-by-step direction cards.

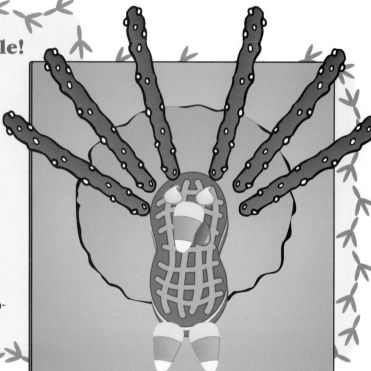

What to Do When the Snack Is Through

Here's a letter-formation activity your youngsters will stick with! Write the following uppercase letters on lined chart paper: *A, E, F, H, I, K, L, M, N, T, V, W, X, Y, Z.* (Make each letter two lines tall.) Place the chart paper on a table along with any extra pretzel sticks. Invite your little ones to form each letter by placing the pretzel sticks on top of the letters on the chart paper. For older students, display the chart paper in a prominent place, and encourage the children to use the pretzel sticks to form the letters on a tabletop.

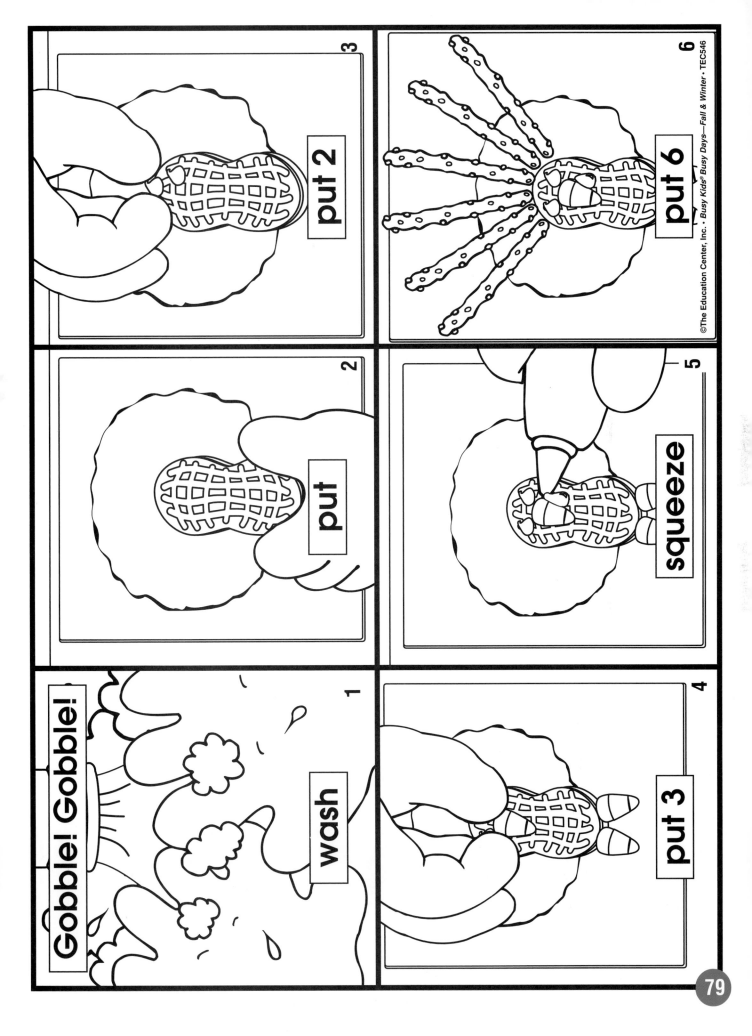

put 2

put 6

put

squeeze

Gobble! Gobble!

wash

put 3

©The Education Center, Inc. • Busy Kids® Busy Days—Fall & Winter • TEC546

Thanksgiving

Turkey Tail Tune

Invite little ones to count up and down on their fingers to this popular tune. But first, enlist ten volunteers to help make an accordion book to add to the feathery fun. Ask each child to draw a featherless turkey on a sheet of construction paper. Label each page with a numeral from 1 to 10. Then have each child glue the corresponding number of construction paper feathers to her turkey body. Sequence and tape the pages together to create an accordion-style book. Add a title and laminate the book for durability. Then use the book while singing the song. Be sure to encourage youngsters to hold up the appropriate number of fingers as they sing and count along.

(sung to the tune of "Ten Little Indians")

One little, two little, three little feathers,
Four little, five little, six little feathers,
Seven little, eight little, nine little feathers,
Ten bright turkey feathers.

Ten little, nine little, eight little feathers,
Seven little, six little, five little feathers,
Four little, three little, two little feathers,
One bright turkey feather.

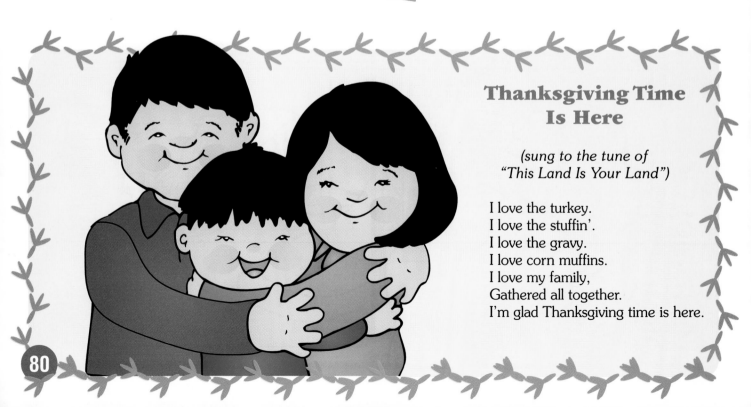

Thanksgiving Time Is Here

(sung to the tune of "This Land Is Your Land")

I love the turkey.
I love the stuffin'.
I love the gravy.
I love corn muffins.
I love my family,
Gathered all together.
I'm glad Thanksgiving time is here.

Two Tom Turkeys

Add some gobblin' good fun to this turkey rhyme with these simple finger puppets. To create the puppets, use a red washable pen to draw a turkey head on the tips of each child's index fingers.

Two tom turkeys	*Hold up both index fingers.*
Sitting on a fence.	
One named Arthur.	*Wiggle left index finger.*
One named Spence.	*Wiggle right index finger.*
Run away, Arthur!	*Bounce left index finger to the side.*
Danger is near.	
Run away, Spence!	*Bounce right index finger to the side.*
Thanksgiving Day is here!	
Two tom turkeys	*Hold both index fingers behind back.*
Hiding far away,	
Waiting for the end	
Of Thanksgiving Day.	
Come back, Arthur.	*Bounce left index finger to front of body.*
Come back, Spence.	*Bounce right index finger to front of body.*
It's safe to come back	
And sit on the fence!	*Wiggle index fingers together.*

Gobble, Gobble, Giggle

I'm a little turkey here to say,
"Try some beef on Thanksgiving Day.
Turkey is tough, and turkey is dry.
You really should give chicken a try!
Or how 'bout a plate of veggie delight
For a Thanksgiving dinner that tastes just right?"

Thanksgiving

The Tasty Thanksgiving Feast: A Lift-the-Flap Book

The Tasty Thanksgiving Feast: A Lift-the-Flap Book by Suzy-Jane Tanner (HarperCollins Publishers, Inc.) is sure to satisfy your young-sters' appetites for a good story. Discuss how each of Henrietta's friends contributed something to their Thanksgiving feast. Then follow up your reading with this critical-thinking activity. To prepare, gather several Thanksgiving feast–related items, such as a fork or spoon, a can of cranberry sauce, a can of pumpkin pie filling, a magazine pic-ture of a roasted turkey, an empty box of stuffing mix, a squash, and an ear of corn. Place the items in a paper grocery bag. Place one item in a basket and cover the top of the basket with a festive cloth napkin. After sharing Tanner's story, show youngsters the basket and give them clues to help them guess what's under the napkin. After youngsters have had a chance to guess, have a child reveal it for the class. Continue this guessing game with the other items in the bag.

Albert's Thanksgiving

Every time Albert tries to harvest the vegetables for the Thanksgiving feast, Patsy Pig sends a message requesting his help for something else! Will the vegetables ever be ready for the feast? Find out by reading *Albert's Thanksgiving* by Leslie Tryon (Aladdin Paperbacks). After sharing the story with the class, have an adult come to the door delivering a note (like the one shown) and a class supply of large, round sugar cookies. Read the note to the class. Then take out a tray of these ingre-dients: sweetened pumpkin pie filling, whipped cream, and chocolate chips (or raisins). Invite youngsters to spread the sweetened pumpkin pie filling on their cookies (pizza crusts), spoon on some whipped cream, and top off the pizzas with chocolate chips. Once the pizzas are done, pretend it's time for the feast and dig in!

Dear Class,
    Today is our annual Thanksgiving feast. Patsy Pig has given me so many jobs that I just can't find the time to make pumpkin pizza pies this year. Could you please make your own to bring to the feast? Thanks so much for your help.

    Albert

P.S. I have sent the crusts to help you get started.

The smallest member of the family feels left out of the Thanksgiving preparations, until Grandpa steps in and suggests they gather chestnuts together in *Thanksgiving Treat* by Catherine Stock (Aladdin Paperbacks). Gather (or purchase) some chestnuts of your own to share with the class. Cut a few chestnuts open, and invite youngsters to observe the meat inside. If possible, show the children a *bur*—the prickly seed case that chestnuts develop in. If a real bur is not available, show little ones the illustration of a bur on the book's title page. Then follow up by taking your class outdoors to search for other nuts or seeds that may have fallen from autumn trees. Encourage youngsters to place nuts and other interesting nature items they collect in your science center for all to observe.

Gracias, the Thanksgiving Turkey

Miguel's father sends him a turkey with instructions to fatten the bird up for Thanksgiving, but Miguel has a different plan in mind for his fine-feathered friend. Read *Gracias, the Thanksgiving Turkey* by Joy Cowley (Scholastic Trade Books) to find out what happens to this lovable turkey. Then give older students a little lesson in Spanish using the Spanish words from the book. Before reading the story, copy the Spanish words listed in the book's glossary onto a sheet of chart paper. (Do not record the English translations yet.) Share the cover and title of the book with the children, and then ask them if they know what the word *gracias* means. Explain that the story features Spanish words that they will learn later. After reading the story once to enjoy the plot, reread the story and encourage youngsters to raise their hands every time they hear a word that sounds Spanish. Encourage the class to use context clues to decipher the meaning of each Spanish word they hear. Then record the English translation on the chart paper. If desired, have the class dictate a note for Miguel's father asking him to spare Gracias's life. Wherever possible, substitute Spanish words from your list in the class note.

Abuela	grandmother
Abuelo	grandfather
amiga	friend (girl)
amigos	friends
Gracias	thank you
hijo	son
loco	crazy

A Turkey for Thanksgiving

Turkey is the guest of honor, not the main course, in *A Turkey for Thanksgiving* by Eve Bunting (Clarion Books). Extend youngsters' enjoyment of this story with a turkey hunt of your own. In advance, make a brown construction paper headband with craft feathers glued to the back. Seat the children in a circle; then ask one student volunteer to close his eyes (or wear a blindfold) while you quietly send another volunteer off to a hidden area of the room wearing the headband. When the turkey is safely hidden, ask the first volunteer to open his eyes and look at the circle of children to determine the identity of the hidden turkey. Once he has figured it out, have him retrieve the turkey from her hiding place and invite her to Thanksgiving dinner (back to the circle). Repeat the game until all your little turkeys have had a chance to participate.

Fairy Tales

Our Favorite Good Guys and Gals

Cinderella | the prince | pig #3

Favorite Good Guys and Gals

Count on the good guys for this graphing activity! Select three fairy tales that feature a positive hero or heroine, such as Cinderella, the prince in *Sleeping Beauty,* and the third pig in *The Three Little Pigs.* Title a sheet of chart paper "Our Favorite Good Guys and Gals." Divide the paper into three columns; then draw and label one of the three characters you've chosen at the base of each column. After reading the three stories, discuss each chosen character's traits and why he or she was good. Next ask each child to decide which of the three characters is his favorite; then give him a sticky dot to place in the corresponding column. When the graph is complete, have the class count the dots to discover which good guy (or gal) is the class favorite.

A Fine Vine

Use Jack's beanstalk to cultivate counting skills. To begin, color and cut out a tagboard copy of climbing Jack on page 198. Also cut a long strip of green poster board. Draw a simple vine on the strip. Laminate the vine and boy cutouts for durability. Punch a hole near the top and bottom of the vine. Cut a length of green yarn twice as long as the vine. Thread the yarn through the holes; then tape the yarn ends together to create a movable loop. Tape Jack to the yarn loop at the bottom of the vine. Then, starting at the bottom, use a wipe-off marker to write the numerals 1 through 10 at evenly spaced intervals up the vine. (For students with more advanced counting skills, write the numerals 1 through 20.)

To use, pull the yarn loop (from the back of the vine) to make Jack climb the beanstalk. Invite youngsters to count along as Jack passes each numeral. Then pull the yarn in the opposite direction to make Jack climb back down. Have students count backward as Jack makes his way to the bottom. See how Jack's fine vine makes a fine counting line!

Tongue-Twistin' Tale Titles

Tickle youngsters' funny bones with this laughable language activity. To begin, write the title of a familiar fairy tale on a sheet of chart paper. Read the title to the class; then cover the first letter (or blend) in each key word with a small sticky note. Ask a child to name a consonant. Write the uppercase version of that letter on each sticky note. Then challenge youngsters to read the new fairy-tale title. For example, *Little Red Riding Hood* might be retitled *Bittle Bed Biding Bood* or *Hansel and Gretel* might become *Mansel and Metel*. These ticklish, tongue-twistin' titles will create a flurry of fairy-tale fun!

Simmering Stone Soup

After reading your favorite version of *Stone Soup,* cook up some counting and letter-identification skills with this recipe. To prepare, draw a chart as shown. Put the chart, the ingredients, measuring spoons, and a class supply of plastic bowls and spoons in your cooking center. Invite each child in a small group to follow the chart, counting out vegetables into his own bowl. Have him measure a teaspoon of alphabet pasta into his bowl. Challenge him to name some of the pasta letters in his mixture.

When all the groups have prepared their ingredients, gather the class to reenact the story and make your own stone soup. First put the "stone" into a large pot. Ask each child if he has something to contribute; then invite him to add his pasta-vegetable mix to the pot. Finally, add the vegetable juice and enough water to cover the vegetables. Cook the soup until the vegetables are heated through. Enjoy the tasty results!

Stone Soup
1 stone (chicken bouillon cube)
3 canned carrot slices (per child)
7 frozen peas (per child)
10 frozen corn kernels (per child)
1 teaspoon alphabet pasta (per child)
large can of vegetable juice
water

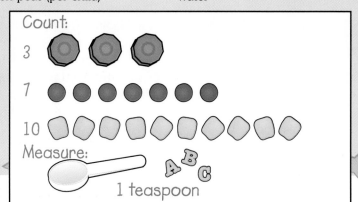

Run, Gingerbread Man!

Let this gingerbread man help youngsters run away with valuable left-to-right reading skills. To make a pointer, trace a gingerbread-man cookie cutter onto a sheet of brown craft foam. Cut out the shape; then add features to the cutout using craft items, such as sequins and rickrack ribbon. Tape the foam cutout to a ruler. Then write the following on chart paper: "Run, run, run as fast as you can. You can't catch me. I'm the Gingerbread Man." (Or copy the character's exact words from your favorite version of the classic fairy tale.) Once students are familiar with the story, read the chart to your class. As you read, show youngsters how to "run" the gingerbread-man pointer under the words. Then retell the story. Each time you reach the gingerbread man's speaking part, have a volunteer lead the class in reciting the part as he runs the pointer under the words on the chart.

Fairy Tales

Royal Role-Play

Crown each child king or queen for some royal role-playing in the block center. To prepare, cover several tagboard crowns with aluminum foil; then staple the queen and king cards from a deck of playing cards to the crowns. Put the crowns and a few robes in your block center, along with some paper-towel-tube scepters. Invite youngsters in the center to dress as royalty; then have them construct a castle from blocks to house the royal family. Encourage the small groups of children to act out a regal fairy tale with the aid of their props. If desired, take photos to create a display showing off your youngsters' majestic imaginations.

Fairy-Tale Detectives

Stimulate youngsters' thinking skills with the push of a button—the button on your tape recorder, that is! To prepare for this listening-center activity, gather three fairy-tale books familiar to your children. Select several lines from the text of each tale that provide clues to the story. (Avoid choosing lines that include the title.) Make a tape recording of the chosen lines, using a bell to signal the end of the clues for each fairy tale. Place the tape and the three books in the listening center. Invite your little ones to listen carefully to the recording to identify the book corresponding to each set of clues. Then challenge youngsters to put the books in the order in which they heard the clues on the tape. (For younger students, you may want to include very specific directions on the tape, such as, "Those are all the clues for this story. Can you find this book?")

Going on a Bean Hunt

Youngsters will dig this sand-and-bean activity. To prepare, pour a bag of large dried beans (such as lima beans) into your sand table; then cover the beans with sand. Provide sifters, shovels, rakes, and a few miniature clay pots. After sharing *Jack and the Beanstalk* with your youngsters, explain that some of the beans landed right in your sand table when Jack's mother threw them out the window! Then have students in this center use the various tools to hunt for the beans and collect them in the pots. Invite each child to count the beans he finds.

Trip-Trap Over the Bridge

Invite youngsters to role-play this troll play from *The Three Billy Goats Gruff*. In the block area, provide three goats from a toy farm set and one toy troll. Have small groups of children construct the troll's bridge from blocks. (If desired, invite your youngsters to build the bridge over a large tray of water.) When the bridge is complete, prompt the children to trip-trap their goats over the bridge in their own versions of this delightful tale.

A Tale of Numbers

Here's a math activity that your youngsters are sure to think is number one! Prepare a tape recording of simple math problems based on various fairy tales. Begin the recording with the rhyme below; then follow the rhyme with a clue, such as, "The big bad wolf blew down this many houses." After a brief pause, repeat the rhyme followed by a different clue. Place the tape, a set of numeral cards labeled from 1–10, and a collection of corresponding fairy tales in your math center.

Invite student pairs to listen to each rhyme and clue on the tape. Have the children stop the tape after each clue to find the appropriate numeral card. If necessary, encourage youngsters to review the fairy-tale books to help them arrive at the correct answer.

I'm thinking of a number.
What number can it be?
It's in a special fairy tale.
Show that number to me.

Fairy Tales

"Sense-ible" Little Red Riding Hood

Use the story of *Little Red Riding Hood* to reinforce the five senses. Divide your class into two groups. Have one group recite Little Red Riding Hood's lines and the other group say the lines of the wolf disguised as Grandmother (see below). After the last line, have your little wolves jump up to surprise all your Little Red Riding Hoods!

Little Red Riding Hood:	*Wolf:*
"Grandmother, what big eyes you have!"	"The better to see you with, my dear!"
"Grandmother, what big ears you have!"	"The better to hear you with, my dear!"
"Grandmother, what a big nose you have!"	"The better to smell you with, my dear!"
"Grandmother, what big hands you have!"	"The better to touch you with, my dear!"
"Grandmother, what big teeth you have!"	*"The better to eat you with!"*

Fairy-Tale Association

Challenge your little ones to test their memories with this recall activity. In advance make a simple crown from construction paper. Seat the children in a circle; then name a fairy tale such as *Cinderella*. Pass the crown to the child on your right. Have him put the crown on his head, name one character from *Cinderella,* and then pass the crown to the next person. Continue until no other characters from that fairy tale can be named. Name another fairy tale and start again with the next child in the circle.

Prince Charming!

Name That Tale

When it's time to bring your fairy-tale unit to a close, "high-tale" it with the following verses. Challenge youngsters to identify the tales described in each verse. If desired, make up more verses for your other favorite fairy tales.

(sung to the tune of "Row, Row, Row Your Boat")

Once upon a time,
Two children in a wood
Came upon a candy house,
And, boy, did it look good!
(Hansel and Gretel)

Once upon a time,
A girl all dressed in red
Went to visit her granny,
But found a wolf instead.
(Little Red Riding Hood)

Once upon a time,
There lived a girl so fair.
She paid a visit to a home,
The home of the three bears.
(Goldilocks and the Three Bears)

Magic Counting Beans

Count on Jack's beans to show your students some magical math fun. In advance put ten dried beans, such as lima or kidney beans, into a paper cup for each child. Distribute the cups to the children. Secretly write down a numeral between 1 and 10 on a large piece of tagboard. Ask each child to guess the numeral he thinks is on the tagboard. Then have him count the same number of beans from his cup into the palm of his hand. Reveal the written numeral; then confirm whether any child guessed correctly. You can count on your youngsters wanting to do this again and again!

Snow White and Friends

Lead youngsters in this action poem as you role-play Snow White and her friends.

Bashful, Bashful, hide your face	*Cover face with hands.*
Happy, Happy, dance in place.	*Dance.*
Grumpy, Grumpy, make a frown.	*Frown.*
Dopey, Dopey, turn around.	*Twirl around.*
Sleepy, Sleepy, close your eyes.	*Rest head on clasped hands and close eyes.*
Doc, Doc, you're so wise.	*Tap temple and nod.*
Sneezy, Sneezy, say, "Ah-choo!"	*Pretend to sneeze.*
Snow White sure loves all of you!	*Blow a kiss.*

Fairy Tales

String, String, As Fast As You Can...

Let's make a necklace with a gingerbread man! To prepare, use a small gingerbread-man cookie cutter to trace a class supply of gingerbread men onto craft foam; then cut them out. Next dye a pound of ziti or rigatoni in two cups of rubbing alcohol and five to six drops of food coloring. Spread the pasta out to dry on waxed paper. Then wrap a piece of masking tape around one end of a length of yarn for each child. Place the yarn lengths, the pasta, and a hole puncher in a center.

To make a necklace, a child punches a hole in the top of a foam cutout. Then she counts out ten pieces of pasta. She strings the pasta and gingerbread man onto a length of yarn. Help each child tie the ends of her yarn together to complete her necklace. Youngsters will wear these nifty necklaces happily ever after!

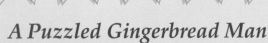

A Puzzled Gingerbread Man

Give a happy ending to *The Gingerbread Man* with these homemade puzzles. To begin, cut out a tagboard gingerbread man for each child. Instruct each child to color his cutout. Then have him cut his gingerbread man into six pieces—a head, a body, two arms, and two legs. Give each child a resealable plastic bag in which to put his puzzle pieces. Then gather your students, with their puzzle bags in hand, to share your favorite version of this classic tale. Before beginning, have each child assemble his puzzle; then read the story. When you get to the part where the fox eats the gingerbread man, have youngsters take their puzzles apart piece by piece. Then, after the fox takes his last gulp, invite students to outfox the fox. Have them quickly put their gingerbread men together again to bring them back to life!

Goldilocks and the Play-Dough Bears

Your youngsters will have a "bear-rel" of fun at this play-dough center! Invite three children at a time to the center. Remind them that in *Goldilocks and the Three Bears,* each bear is a different size. Then have each child decide which of the three bears he will make from play dough. Ask him to roll play-dough balls for each of his bear's body parts—a head, a body, arms, legs, and ears. Then have him assemble the balls into a bear shape. If desired, have him add sequins for facial features. Then provide a female play figure and some dollhouse furniture, such as a table, chairs, and beds. (Or have students create their own play-dough story props.) Invite youngsters to role-play the story with their play-dough bears and the props.

Jack's Magic Beans

Youngsters can convert a bag of Jack's beans into gold with this magical game. To prepare, pour a quantity of gold-wrapped chocolate coins into a large bucket. Then gather a large bowl of dried beans and several clean socks. Instruct each child in a small group to fill a sock halfway with several handfuls of beans; then help her knot the top of the sock to create a beanbag.

To play, place the bucket of gold coins on the floor. Explain that in *Jack and the Beanstalk,* Jack had to face the giant to get gold coins. But each player here can get gold coins with a simple toss of her beanbag—and without the hassles of a giant! Have each student, in turn, stand about three feet from the bucket. Challenge her to toss her beanbag into the bucket. When she hits the target, invite her to reach into the bucket and pull out a gold-coin treat. After several rounds of play, ask each child to undo the knot in her beanbag and return the beans to the bowl. Then invite another group of students to try this toss-and-treat game.

Three Pigs Construction Company

Set up a house-making station where your little ones can try their hands at making houses from straw, sticks, or bricks—and get some practice with fine-motor control at the same time! To prepare, cut a supply of simple house shapes from construction paper. Then cut some raffia into short lengths and some red craft foam into small rectangles. Place the paper houses, the cut raffia (straw), some toothpicks (sticks), the foam rectangles (bricks), and a few bottles of glue in a center.

Invite children who visit this center to glue their choice of materials onto a paper house shape. They may want to choose one type of house or "build" all three.

Fairy Tales

Abracadabra

Use your magic wand to wave a little fairy-tale fantasy over your youngsters. To make a wand, decorate a star cut from construction paper with glitter; then tape the star to a wooden dowel. Then wave your wand over the class and say, "Abracadabra, Bibbully Baracter, I now turn you into this fairy-tale character. You are [name of character]." Assign a character mentioned below, and ask youngsters to do the suggested movement.

Character	Movement
Cinderella	Dance with a partner at the ball.
Sleeping Beauty	Sleep on the floor.
Hansel & Gretel	Skip through the forest with a partner.
The Gingerbread Man	Run as fast as you can.
Billy Goat Gruff	Walk over a bridge (balance beam).

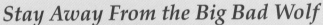

Stay Away From the Big Bad Wolf

This reenactment of *The Three Little Pigs* will have you and your little ones huffing, puffing, and giggling! Gather three large bed sheets; then spread them on the grass in an open field. Tell your youngsters that you are going to play the part of the Big Bad Wolf while they play the part of the Little Pigs. Have all the pigs hide under the first sheet. After asking the pigs to let you in, pretend to huff, puff, and blow their house in by pulling the sheet off the pigs. Have the pigs run to the next sheet, then hide under it. Have them pretend to go to sleep for the night. After a few moments, repeat your part; then direct the pigs to hide under the last sheet. Walk several feet away; then have the pigs come out to go to the fair. (Have students walk to and from a designated area.) As the pigs are walking home from the fair, begin to chase them. Encourage the pigs to roll on the ground like butter churns to frighten the Wolf away!

A Castle for a King

Mold some fairy-tale magic into your sandbox with castles fit for a king! Gather spray bottles filled with water, several sand shovels, and molding materials such as funnels, cookie cutters, sand pails, and paper cups. Divide the class into groups of three to four children; then have each group gather around a corner of your outdoor sandbox. (If you don't have a sandbox, divide two bags of sand from your local hardware store among a few large plastic tubs.) Pass out a spray bottle to each group and have youngsters take turns moistening the sand. Provide an equal number of shovels and molding materials for each group to begin its castle creation. Encourage students to gather rocks and sticks to adorn their castles. Watch as your youngsters turn the sandbox into a magical kingdom right before your eyes!

Cinderella's Chores

Cleaning up is fun when you pretend to be Cinderella! Set up four Cinderella cleaning stations on a blacktop or concrete area. At the dishwashing station, provide a few sponges, a dishpan of sudsy water, and plastic dishware. At the sweeping station, place a few brooms and a dustpan. Put two or more feather dusters and a chair (for dusting) at the third station. At the fourth station, provide a bucket of water and two or more rags for scrubbing the blacktop.

When the stations are prepared, divide your class into small groups and assign each group to a station. Set youngsters to work sweeping, scrubbing, dusting, and washing dishes. Rotate the groups around the stations until everyone has had a chance to do every chore. Your little Cinderellas are sure to have a ball!

Little Red on the Run

Enthusiasm will be riding high with this game of Run, Red, Run! To prepare, cut four small flowers from construction paper for each pair of children in your class. Then make enough paper-bag baskets for half the class. To make a basket, staple a two-inch construction-paper strip across the opening of a small paper bag.

Bring your students outdoors; then divide the class into partners. Designate one child in each pair Little Red Riding Hood and the other child the Big Bad Wolf. Spread the flowers in a field; then give each "Red" a basket for collecting four flowers to bring to Granny. Give a starting signal; then encourage each Wolf to chase and tag his partner before she gathers her flowers. If Little Red Riding Hood gets tagged before gathering all four flowers, the partners trade roles. If not, she replaces the flowers and continues on as Little Red Riding Hood until she is captured by the Wolf.

Got ya, "Little Red"!

Fairy Tales

Magic Wand

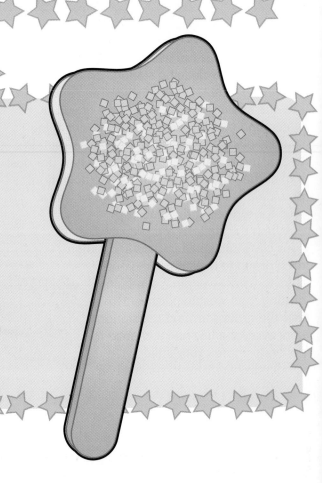

Ingredients:
1 slice of toast per child
melted butter
blue sugar sprinkles

Utensils and Supplies:
1 jumbo craft stick per child
napkins
star-shaped cookie cutter
pastry brush

Teacher Preparation:
Toast a slice of bread for each child. Melt the butter. Arrange the ingredients and utensils near the step-by-step direction cards.

Dear boys and girls,

Here's some candy for you from my house. Hansel and Gretel enjoyed it, and I know you will, too!

Your friend,
Wanda Witch

What to Do When the Snack Is Through

Don't toss those toast scraps! Use them for acting out a fun twist to the story of *Hansel and Gretel*. Tear the toast scraps into small pieces. Before school one day, make a winding trail of bread crumbs outdoors, leading from your classroom (or building) to another location at your school or center. Leave a box of wrapped candy at the end of the trail, along with the note shown. When youngsters arrive, point out the bread-crumb trail and invite them to follow it. Surprise!

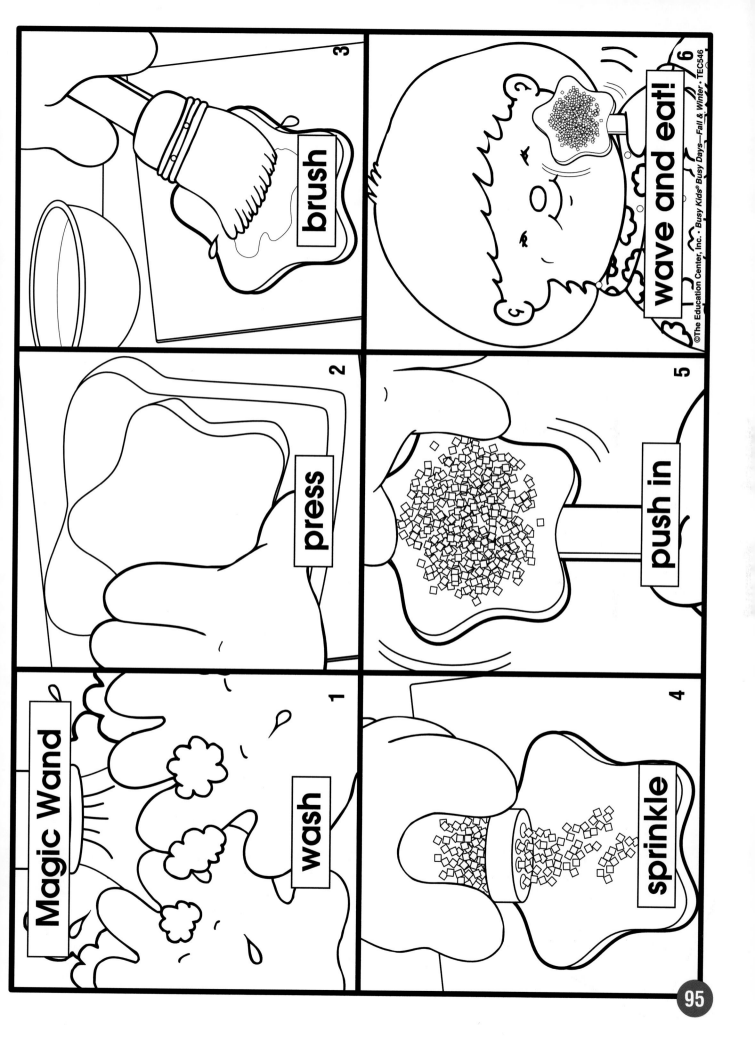

©The Education Center, Inc. • Busy Kids® Busy Days—Fall & Winter • TEC546

Fairy Tales

Once Upon a Time

Sing this lively tune at the start of your circle time or storytime during each day of your Fairy-Tales unit.

(sung to the tune of "Here Comes Peter Cottontail")

"Once upon a time," they say.
Fairy tales begin that way.
Those stories take me to a magic land.
"Once upon a time," they say.
Fairy tales begin that way.
I could read fairy tales every day!

Three Pigs Action Song

(sung to the tune of "My Hat, It Has Three Corners")

[Three] pigs,	*Hold up three fingers.*
They have [three] houses.	*Make roof with hands.*
[Three] houses	*Make roof with hands.*
Have [three] pigs.	*Hold up three fingers.*
But when wolf	*Hold hands against head for wolf ears.*
Huffs and "puff-es,"	*Blow.*
The [straw] house	*Make roof with hands.*
Blows right down.	*Part hands and hold out to sides.*

Repeat verse, replacing the word three *with* two *and the word* straw *with* stick. *Hold up two fingers at the appropriate times. Then sing the following final verse.*

One pig,	*Hold up one finger.*
He has one brick house.	*Make roof with hands.*
One brick house	*Make roof with hands.*
Has one pig.	*Show one finger.*
And though wolf	*Hold hands against head for wolf ears.*
Huffs and "puff-es,"	*Pause and blow hard.*
His house	*Make roof with hands.*
Does not blow down!	*Shake head.*

Little Red Hen

(sung to the tune of "Shortnin' Bread")

"My friends, will you help me?"
    asked Little Red Hen.
"Friends, will you help me [plant
    this wheat]?"
"Not I," said the dog. "Not I," said
    the cat.
"Not I," said the mouse. "Do it
    yourself!"

Repeat the verse three more
times. In sequence, replace the underlined words with *cut this
wheat, mill this wheat,* or *make
this bread.* Then sing the last
verse as follows.

"My friends, will you help me?"
    asked Little Red Hen.
"Friends, will you help me eat this
    bread?"
"I will!" said the dog. "I will!" said
    the cat.
"I will!" said the mouse. But Red
    Hen said—

(spoken) "No thanks! I'll eat it
    myself!"

Guess Who in Fairy-Tale Land?

Use this song to encourage your
fairy-tale detectives to solve these
"Once upon a time" mysteries.

*(sung to the tune of "Who's
Afraid of the Big Bad Wolf?")*

Guess who had the [glass slipper],
[Glass slipper],
[Glass slipper].
Guess who had the [glass slipper].
Name the character.

Each time you repeat the song,
insert a different item from a familiar
fairy tale, such as *house of bricks,
tall beanstalk,* or *broken chair.*

Just Kidding Around

After reading *The Three Billy Goats
Gruff* to your class, teach youngsters this
musical synopsis of the story.

*(sung to the tune of
"The Bear Went Over the Mountain")*

The goats went over the troll's bridge.
The goats went over the troll's bridge.
The goats went over the troll's bridge,
To reach the green, green grass.

The troll wanted to eat the goats.
The troll wanted to eat the goats.
The troll wanted to eat the goats,
But they knocked him off the bridge.

97

Fairy Tales

The Ugly Duckling

Read aloud Jerry Pinkney's adaptation of *The Ugly Duckling* (Morrow Junior Books) for a thought-provoking lesson in acceptance. (You may want to read the story in two sessions for younger students.) Retold in a sensitive yet dramatic way, this timeless classic will prompt discussion about how our treatment of others can either hurt or heal. As you read the story, pause and ask for comments whenever the duckling is mistreated. Help youngsters verbalize how they think the ugly ducking is feeling and why. After the story, ask your little ones to share examples of times when they have felt excluded or different. In addition, discuss circumstances that have made your youngsters feel good. Divide a sheet of chart paper into two columns, labeled as shown. Brainstorm together a list of words or phrases that fit each category. In the following days, encourage children to use the positive words (or phrases) from your list when interacting with their classmates.

○ Words That Hurt	○ Words That Heal
You can't play.	Want to play with us?
I don't like you anymore.	I like your picture.
You look funny.	I like your dress.
I don't want to be your friend.	Will you be my friend?

Little Red Hen to Go

The Little Red Hen

Its simple text and cheerful illustrations make Byron Barton's version of *The Little Red Hen* (HarperCollins Children's Books) a fairy-tale delight. Read the story several times to familiarize the children with the characters and plot. As a follow-up, photocopy a class supply of the animals on page 201 onto heavy paper. Give each child a copy. Encourage him to color the animals and then cut them apart. Have him make the animals into puppets by taping them to craft sticks. Provide small paper bags for storing the puppets, and write "Little Red Hen to Go" on the outside of each bag. Reread the story to the class. As each animal is featured, encourage youngsters to hold up the matching puppet. Also encourage youngsters to recite the characters' predictable lines. Continue having students participate in readings until they can use the puppets to tell the tale on their own. Then send the bags home so students can perform it for family and friends.

The Elves and the Shoemaker

Sew a little magic into your day with a reading of *The Elves and the Shoemaker*, retold by Bernadette Watts (North-South Books Inc.). As an extension, invite your little elves to strengthen their fine-motor skills by "sewing" shoes. In advance, trace a shoe onto brown craft foam; then cut out the shoe. Use a hole puncher to make evenly spaced holes around the edge of the foam shoe. Knot one end of a length of black lanyard (or yarn) to one hole in the shoe. (If using yarn, dip the loose end in glue and let it dry.) Make a desired number of shoes in the same manner and place them at a center. Invite your little cobblers to come to the workbench and sew some shoes. Show them how to weave the lacing in and out of each hole in a shoe. They're sure to have fun, right down to the very last stitch!

The Tortoise and the Hare

You'll have little ones on their feet at the conclusion of *The Tortoise and the Hare* as they discover who wins the race between the pokey tortoise and his over-confident opponent. Use this Aesop fable, retold by Janet Stevens (Holiday House, Inc.), to teach youngsters the importance of showing effort even in times of doubt. In advance, make a tortoise pin by hot-gluing half of a walnut shell to a tortoise-shaped background cut from green felt. Glue wiggle eyes to the head. When the glue is dry, hot-glue a safety pin to the back of the tortoise. After reading the story, discuss how Tortoise showed effort even though he didn't think he could win the race. Then seat youngsters in a circle and pass around the tortoise pin. As each child holds the tortoise, encourage her to say, "I was like Tortoise when…" and describe a personal experience when she tried hard and accomplished her goal. Responses might include learning to cut with scissors, ride a bike, or tie shoes. In the following days, pin the tortoise to a child's clothing when she exhibits excellent effort, just as Tortoise did.

The Gingerbread Man

After a reading of Barbara Baumgartner's simple version of *The Gingerbread Man* (Dorling Kindersley Publishing, Inc.), invite little ones to make their own gingerbread men from some spicy-smelling play dough. Mix up a batch of your favorite play dough, adding food coloring to make it brown and two tablespoons of ground ginger to scent it. Give each child in a small group a portion of dough on a square of waxed paper. Encourage the children to roll their dough into snake shapes. Then have them form the snakes into shapes to make the body parts of a gingerbread man, such as a circle for a head, a rectangle for a body, and four ovals to make the arms and legs. If desired, provide raisins and M&M's® candies so little ones can add faces and buttons to their gingerbread creations.

Friends

Count On Friends

Here's a picture-perfect way to teach youngsters that they can count on friends. With a new roll of film in your camera, take a picture of a student volunteer; then invite her to choose a friend to include in a second photo. After snapping the second picture, ask the second child to invite a friend to join the group. Take a picture of the trio; then have the third child bring another friend to the group. Continue in this manner, adding a friend to the existing group for each new photo, until every child is pictured in the last photo. (Make sure all the children are clearly visible in every photo.) Mount each picture onto a tagboard card; then laminate the cards, if desired. Draw a number line on a long strip of bulletin board paper, ending with the total number of children in your class. Then randomly distribute the pictures to students. Have each child count the friends in his picture; then have him tape his photo onto the number line. You can count on friends!

Just Call On Me

A friend is just a phone call away. And when your little ones dial their friends at this center, they will also be calling on their number skills! To begin, make a student telephone directory. Glue each child's class photo onto a notecard; then write her name and telephone number on the card. Laminate each card for durability. Punch two holes at the top of each card and then bind the cards with two metal rings. Place a student desk, the directory, a play telephone, a notepad, and pencils in a center. A child at this center finds a friend's card in the directory. He copies the phone number on the notepad. Then he dials his friend for a casual chat about this or that. Hello, friend!

A Rhyme for a Friend

Keep friends gigglin' together with this rhymin' good time that promotes phonemic awareness. Seat your little ones in a circle. Explain that you will say a silly chant about a friend in the class. Challenge youngsters to listen to the rhyming clue and then guess the name of the child. As you chant the second line, replace the beginning sound of the child's name with another sound. Then pause in the next-to-last line to prompt students to fill in the correct name. Repeat the chant several times using different students' names. Then invite each child, in turn, to recite this rollicking rhyme.

I have a friend
Whose name rhymes
    with [Bim].
Hey la-di, la-di, la!
I have a friend.
My friend's name is [Jim].
Hey la-di, la-di, la!

A Snack to Share

Caring means sharing among friends. So share this snack as a surefire way to bring friends together. In advance, gather plastic resealable bags and a few different kinds of snack foods, such as Goldfish® crackers, raisins, Cheerios® cereal, and pretzels. Pour each snack into a separate bowl. Divide the class into pairs; then give each pair a plastic bag. Invite each pair of friends to cooperatively count ten of each snack item into its bag. Once the counting is complete, have the pair distribute the snack items evenly between the partners. Then, as youngsters snack together, share some friendly remarks about their cooperative spirits.

My Friend's Name

In a child's world, his name and his friends' names are of utmost importance. Use youngsters' natural interest in names and these nifty name cards to reinforce name and letter skills. To prepare, glue a small photograph of each child onto a separate notecard; then label the card with the child's name (in capital or lowercase letters, to match your magnetic letters). Laminate the cards for durability. Then back each card with a piece of magnetic tape. Place the cards, a magnetboard, and a set of magnetic letters in a center. To use, a child places a name card on the board. Then he uses the letters to spell the name on the card.

As an added challenge, when you visit this center, ask the child to look away as you remove a magnetic letter from the name he's spelled or add a letter to it. Then challenge the child to find the spelling change in his friend's name.

Friends

Painting Partners

Pair friends together as painting partners to double the fun of an ordinary fingerpainting activity. At the easel or art center, give each set of partners one large sheet of fingerpaint paper and a variety of fingerpaint colors. Encourage each pair to create one colorful work of art together. After the paintings dry, have each pair cut its painting in half so that each partner can take home a reminder of the fun shared between friends.

Paper-Doll Pals

Help youngsters identify their chain of friends with this fine-motor activity. For each child, fold a 9" x 18" piece of construction paper into thirds, so that it measures 9" x 6" folded. Trace a tagboard cutout of the paper-doll pattern (page 202) onto each folded paper as shown. Invite older students to cut around the outline, being careful not to cut through the arm folds. For younger students, cut out the patterns, creating a string of three paper dolls for each child. Invite each child to color each of her paper dolls to resemble a different classmate. Help her label each doll with the corresponding classmate's name. Send each child home with her paper-doll pals to introduce to her mom and dad.

Friendly Letters

The friendly notes written at this stationery factory are bound to manufacture some smiles. To prepare, take a close-up snapshot of each child's face. Photocopy the pictures; then cut them apart. Place the photocopied faces in the writing center; then add envelopes, stamps, stickers, and other decorating items to the center. Invite each child to create a sheet of customized stationery by decorating the outside edges of a sheet of paper with the provided supplies. Then encourage him to write (or dictate or draw) a note to a classmate on the stationery. Have him fold his note, insert it into an envelope, and then seal the envelope. Instruct the child to address the note by gluing the recipient's photocopied photo onto the front of the envelope. Then invite him to deliver the letter to his friend. After all your youngsters visit this center, each child will have written and received a friendly line. What a letter-perfect way to encourage writing—and smiles!

Listening to a "Lotto" Friends

Strengthen listening skills year-round with this friendly lotto game. Or use the game to help youngsters learn classmates' names at the beginning of the year. To begin, tape-record one child at a time saying, "Hi, preschool (or kindergarten) friends! Can you guess which friend I am?" Pause several seconds and then have the child record his name. To create a gameboard, glue individual student photographs onto a small poster board; then laminate the board. Place the gameboard and some bingo chips (or beans) in the listening center. To play, a child listens to each classmate's introduction on the tape. Then he puts a bingo chip on the photo of the child he believes to be the speaker. Can he guess the mystery classmate before that child reveals his name on the tape? In this game, a "lotto" friends turns into a "lotto" fun!

The Foundation of Friendship

Use your block area to build a foundation for friendship through cooperation. Make a circle in the block center with yarn or a plastic hoop. Assign a small number of children to cooperatively build a block structure inside the circle. Be sure to praise the cooperation of the builders as they work together. When the structure is complete, ask the architects to describe their structure to their classmates. Then take a photo of the builders with their creation. Label the photo with the names of the featured children. After you have captured every team of builders on film, display all the photos on a bulletin board titled "Building Friendships With Cooperation."

Friends

Friendship Bears

This flannelboard activity "bears" repeating! In advance, cut five simple bear shapes from each of two different colors of felt. During circle time, tell a friendship story that emphasizes the concept of patterning. For example, "A group of bear friends went hiking. A red bear led the group. A blue bear was second. A red bear was third, and a blue bear was fourth." As you tell the story, have student volunteers put the felt bears on a flannelboard in the order described. Ask youngsters to review the pattern; then have more children continue the pattern using all the bears. Continue by describing other friendly outings, such as the bear friends lining up for a movie or ice cream.

Circle of Friends

Invite your youngsters to create a circle of friends. To prepare, gather a number of different wallpaper samples equal to half the children in your class. Make a tagboard pattern of a person; then use it to trace and cut two people from each wallpaper sample. Before circle time, distribute the wallpaper cutouts. Instruct each child to find the classmate who has the matching cutout and sit next to him in the circle. Once the pairs are seated, demonstrate how to interview a partner by asking a designated question such as, "What is your favorite color?" Then have each friendly pair introduce each other and share the results of the interview.

Each day during your friendship unit, repeat this activity with new pairs and different interview questions.

The Teacher's Friend

Invite an adult friend of yours to come to your classroom and sing the praises of friendship. Have your youngsters sit in a semicircle; then sit beside your friend in the front. Talk about how you met. Tell a favorite story about your friendship. If possible, show photographs of special moments you've shared together. Discuss the importance of listening, laughing, and forgiving in a friendship. Lessons about friendship will come naturally, and children will be delighted to discover that teachers can be good friends, too.

Paper Pals

Keep eyes and ears on you as you snip your way through this story with a surprise ending. In advance fold a 6" x 18" piece of construction paper in half twice so that it measures 4 1/2" x 6". Draw a simple paper-doll figure on the folded paper as shown, making sure the arms go off the edges of the paper. As you begin, keep the drawing facing you and the blank side facing the children. Starting at one leg, begin to slowly cut along the lines of the doll as you make up a story about an imaginary child on her first day of school. Tell about the child meeting classmates on the school playground and at centers. Be certain not to cut apart the folds. As you complete cutting the doll from paper, wrap up the story by telling how the child had made many new friends by the end of the day. Then unfold the paper to display a row of paper pals!

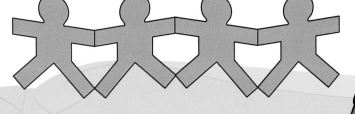

Friendly Faces

Help little ones get to know names and faces with this memory game. Seat all the children in a circle; then have an adult helper escort one child out of sight and out of earshot from the rest of the class. Quietly direct another child in the circle to hide himself in a designated spot. Invite the first child back into the circle; then chant the following:

Friends, friends, one, two, three.
Someone is hiding—
Who can it be?

Give the child a moment to scan her classmates and decide who is hiding. If she is uncertain, give clues until she is successful. After the hidden child reveals himself, begin the game again with two new players.

Where's Rodney?

Friends

A String of Friends

String together a token of friendship with these special necklaces. For each child, dip one end of a 24-inch length of yarn into glue; then let the yarn dry overnight. Cut a supply of large straws into one-inch lengths. Then die-cut a large supply of paper hearts and punch a hole in the center of each one. Give each child an equal number of hearts. Have the child decorate one side of each heart with markers; then have him write his name on the back of each one. Put each child's hearts in a separate egg-carton section. Then put the cut straws, the yarn lengths, and the egg cartons on a table. For each child in a small group, tape the unglued end of a length of yarn to the table.

Invite each child in the first group to select a number of hearts equal to those he decorated, but have him choose hearts decorated by other children. Then have him string his chosen hearts and straw pieces in an alternating pattern onto his yarn. When he finishes, remove the taped end of the yarn from the table; then help the child tie the yarn ends together to create a necklace. Invite him to proudly wear his friendship necklace throughout the day. Then prepare the table for another group of necklace makers.

The Friendship Circle

Put your hands together for friendship by making this friendship wreath. To prepare, cut a large circular wreath from tagboard and a few small hearts from red construction paper. Set up a center with the wreath, construction paper in various skin tones, scissors, and glue. Encourage each child to use his dominant hand to trace his other hand on a paper color of his choice; then have him choose a friend to trace his dominant hand. Help each child cut out his hand tracings. Then have him glue his cutouts onto the tagboard wreath. After all the hand cutouts are glued to the wreath, embellish it with a big red bow and the heart cutouts. This friendship wreath is sure to be a hands-down favorite!

Puzzle Pals

Although friendships can be puzzling at times, these puzzle pals are easy to piece together. To prepare, take a photograph of each child with a few of her friends. Then collect several different tagboard colors. Mount each child's photograph on a half-sheet of tagboard to create a frame around the picture. Laminate the photographs for durability; then cut each photograph into several puzzle pieces. Group the photo puzzles into sets of three, with each puzzle in a set having a different color backing. Then put each puzzle set into a resealable plastic bag. Place the puzzle bags in a center. To use, a child assembles the puzzles in each bag to reunite all the friends. Afterward, she returns the pieces to the appropriate bag for the next child to assemble.

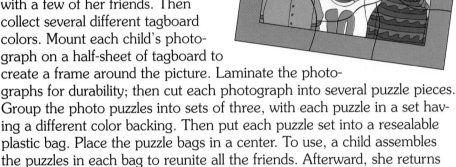

Friend of the Day

Build self-esteem along with fine-motor skills as you highlight the attributes of a true friend. Choose one child each day to be the Friend of the Day. Have that child sit in a special chair in front of the class; then ask the other children to describe why she is a good friend. Give each child a sheet of paper on which to draw the featured friend. Then, on each child's paper, write her dictation about the Friend of the Day, such as "She shares," "She takes turns," or "She helps me clean up." Collect the drawings and bind them together to create a book. Then send the book home with the Friend of the Day. These cherished keepsakes will be permanent reminders of each child's special qualities.

You Gotta Have Friends

Make these friendship snacks as a heartfelt way to spread the true meaning of friendship. To prepare, purchase a container of marshmallow cream, paper towels, and graham crackers. Place the items on a table along with resealable plastic bags, plastic knives, a heart-shaped cookie cutter, and a small rolling pin.

Working with one pair of children at a time, have each child spread a layer of marshmallow cream onto a cracker. Then have the partners place their crackers side by side on a paper towel. Center a cookie cutter atop the crackers where they meet. Then instruct the pair to seal another cracker in a plastic bag. Have the children take turns crushing the cracker with the rolling pin. Then open one side of the bag just a bit so the crumbs can be poured out. Have the partners take turns sprinkling the crumbs into the cookie cutter, covering the marshmallow cream inside it. Then carefully lift the cookie cutter, revealing the cracker-crumb heart. Finally, invite the partners to separate their crackers so that each child gets half of the heart on his cracker. These treats are sure to be "pal-ate" pleasers!

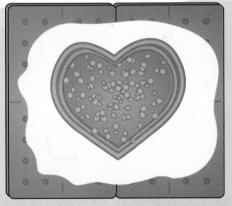

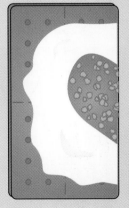

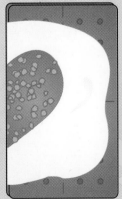

Friends

Circles of Friends

During the first week of school, round up your youngsters for some fast-moving introductions. In an open space, arrange enough plastic hoops on the ground for half of the class. Invite your students to move freely around the hoops as music plays. When you stop the music, direct each child to pair up with a partner inside a hoop. Demonstrate how to introduce yourself by saying, "Hi! My name is [teacher's name]. I am glad to meet you!" Then encourage each child to introduce himself and shake hands with his partner. Invite your youngsters to move to the music again, "hoop-ing" up with a new friend each time the music stops.

My name is Liat, and I like you.

Bounce Into Friendship

At the beginning of the school year when little ones are feeling shy, help them bounce their way into new friendships with this ball game. First have your students stand in a large circle. Holding a large rubber ball, say, "My name is [teacher's name], and I like you, [child's name]." As you say, "I like you," bounce the ball to a student. Have the youngster who catches the ball repeat the sentence using her name, then bounce the ball to a different child. Continue the game until each child has caught and bounced the ball.

Beach-Ball Buddies

Pass along some fun with beach balls. Divide your class into partners and provide each pair with a beach ball. Have the partners stand facing each other. As you play soft music, encourage each pair to pass the ball to each other in a variety of ways. Suggest using two hands, elbows, knees, or feet to pass the ball. Challenge the partners further by asking them to hold the ball steady between their backs or heads. On a final friendly note, ask partners to hold the ball between their stomachs and give each other a hug!

Friendship Challenge

Inflate self-concepts as students use balloons to learn to share and take turns. In advance, inflate enough balloons for half of the class. Divide your class into partners. Give each pair one balloon to share. Challenge partners to keep the balloon in the air without letting it touch the ground. Explain that neither partner should tap the balloon two times in a row. Your students will discover that taking turns and sharing is the key to a successful friendship.

Warning: If a balloon pops, immediately gather up all the pieces. Small pieces of balloon may be a choking hazard.

Special Delivery Postcards

Send some first-class fun with these friendship postcards. Ask each child to use markers and stickers to decorate a large index card. Have each child sign his name on his card; then collect the postcards. Then have your students sit in a large circle to play this mail-delivery game. Place one postcard in a basket that has been decorated with green and yellow ribbon. Give the child whose name is on the card the basket. Have the group sing this version of "A-Tisket, A-Tasket" as the child skips around the circle:

A tisket, a tasket,
A green and yellow basket.
I wrote a letter to my friend,
And on the way I dropped it.

During the last line of the song, have the sender drop the postcard behind a child's back, then run back to his place in the circle. Continue until all youngsters have received a special delivery from a friend!

Friends

Flavorful Friends

Ingredients:
2 vanilla or chocolate wafer cookies per child (purchase one package of each to allow for children's choices)
10 pretzel sticks per child
red, brown, and yellow decorating gel

Utensils and Supplies:
napkins

Teacher Preparation:
Arrange the ingredients and utensils near the step-by-step direction cards.

What to Do When the Snack Is Through

Use any leftover pretzels to help shape up math skills. On separate index cards, draw a triangle, a square, a rectangle, a pentagon, a hexagon, and an octagon. Put the drawings and the extra pretzels at a table. Then invite youngsters to use the pretzels to copy the shapes on the cards.

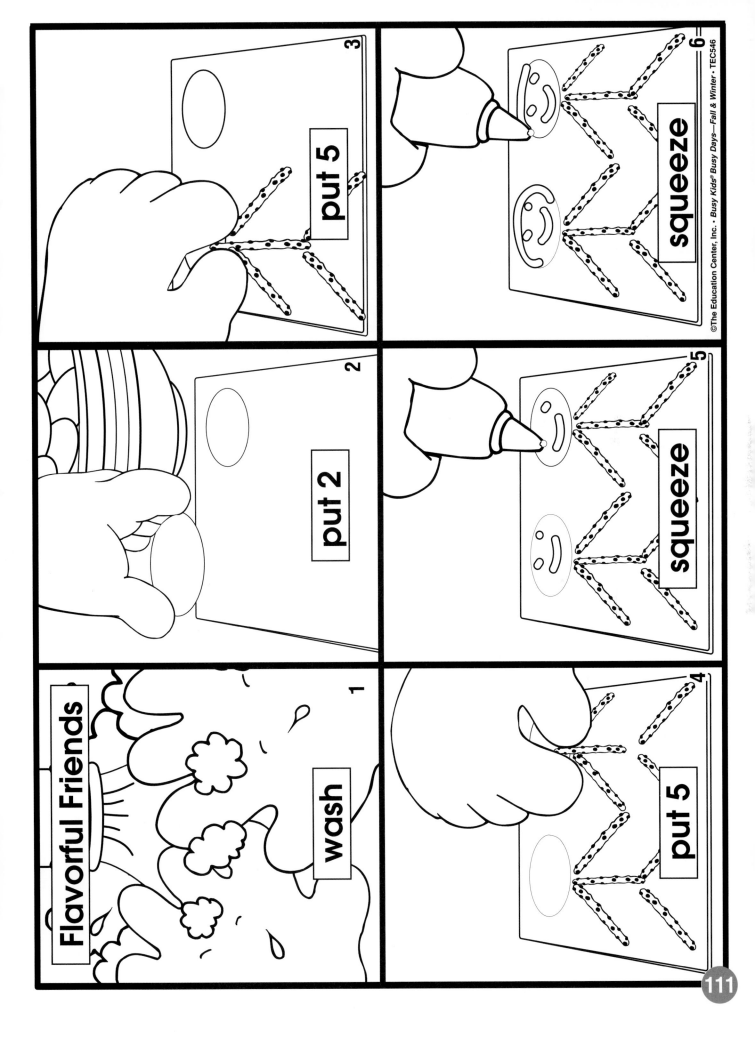

©The Education Center, Inc. • Busy Kids® Busy Days—Fall & Winter • TEC546

Friends

Let Friendship Shine!

Your little friends are sure to shine in the spotlight of this circle activity. In advance, staple yellow crepe paper streamers around a yellow plastic plate to make a sun. Then use a permanent marker to draw a face on the plate. Have the class form a circle; then select a child to stand in the center. Invite her to dance, twirl, and move with the sun as the class sings this tune. Repeat the first verse until each child has had a turn to shine. Then take center stage yourself for the final verse, inviting students to sway their arms over their heads.

(sung to the tune of "This Little Light of Mine")

This little friend of mine, I'm going to let her shine.
This little friend of mine, I'm going to let her shine.
This little friend of mine, I'm going to let her shine.
Let her shine! Let her shine! Let her shine!

These are friends of mine. I'm going to let 'em shine.
These are friends of mine. I'm going to let 'em shine.
These are friends of mine. I'm going to let 'em shine.
Let 'em shine! Let 'em shine! Let 'em shine!

Friends at Play

Five little friends were playing with a ball.   *Hold up five fingers.*
One stopped playing when he heard his momma call,   *Cup hand to ear.*
"Hurry home now, dear. Your supper's getting cold."   *Wave hand toward yourself.*
So the friend ran home as he was told.   *Run one finger behind back.*
Four little friends...
Three little friends...
Two little friends...
One little friend...

No little friends were playing with a ball.   *Make 0 with thumb and fingers.*
They all stopped playing when they heard their mommas call.   *Cup hand to ear.*
Now they're eating supper so it won't get cold.   *Pretend to eat.*
Five friends ran home, just as they were told.   *Hold up five fingers; then nod head.*

A Circle of Friendship

Create a circle of friendship with this song. To begin, seat your little ones in a circle. Sing the song as you walk around the outside of the circle. Take one child's hand at the end of the first line and have her walk around the circle with you. Then invite her to choose a friend at the end of the next line. Continue in this fashion, repeating the song until all the children are a part of the chain. Then close the circle of friendship and sing the song one more time.

(sung to the tune of "Skip to My Lou")

I have a friend. It is you.
I have a friend. It is you.
I have a friend. It is you.
Join our circle of friendship.

Fun With Friends

(sung to the tune of "We Wish You a Merry Christmas")

I'm so glad that you are my friend.
I'm so glad that you are my friend.
I'm so glad that you are my friend,
'Cause you [build blocks] with me.

Repeat the song, replacing the underlined words with one of the following phrases. Or invite your little friends to suggest their own ideas for the last line.

play dolls
ride bikes
share toys

113

Friends

One of Each

Oliver Tolliver learns a valuable lesson about sharing in *One of Each* by Mary Ann Hoberman (Little, Brown and Company). As a follow-up, help your youngsters practice sharing just as Oliver does in the story. Divide your class into pairs; then give each set of friends a banana, a napkin, a pair of scissors, and a plastic knife. Have the class repeat this line from the story, "Why one, simply one, only one, one of each?" Then challenge the friends to figure out a way to enjoy the fruit together. If necessary, direct them to use their scissors to cut the napkin in two and then use their knife to cut the fruit in two. Then remind them of Oliver's words of wisdom: "Eating with friends was the best thing of all. "

To you, my friend,
My hand I give.
We are best friends,
Wherever we live.
Glenda

We Are Best Friends

Read aloud *We Are Best Friends* by Aliki (William Morrow & Company, Inc.) to show youngsters that best friends can remain close even if one has to move away. Invite youngsters who have been separated from a friend to discuss how it made them feel. Then reinforce the idea that best friends can be friends forever by making these special friendship cards. In advance, copy the poem shown and duplicate it for each child. Trim off the excess paper around each copy. Provide youngsters with 9" x 12" construction paper, crayons, and scissors. Have each child fold her paper in half and then place one hand on the paper with her wrist on the fold. Help her trace around her hand; then have her cut around the outline through both thicknesses of paper to create a card made in the shape of her hand. Encourage her to decorate the card's cover and glue the poem to the inside of the card. After she signs her name, send the card home in an envelope to be addressed and sent to a dear friend. Note: *Best Friends Together Again* by Aliki (Greenwillow) is an uplifting sequel to this book.

Mouse	Mole	Otter	Raccoon
neat	messy	too wild	laughs when Cat falls down
likes same games			

Wanted: Best Friend

In *Wanted: Best Friend* by A. M. Monson (Dial Books for Young Readers), Mouse is just the right kind of best friend for Cat. After reading aloud this comical story about friendship, ask youngsters to describe the characteristics of a best friend. Discuss how Cat learns the hard way that true friendship involves some give-and-take. Then divide a sheet of chart paper into four columns. At the top of the first column, write "Mouse." Then list together the reasons why Mouse is the right kind of best friend for Cat. For example, he is neat, unselfish, respectful, and forgiving, and he shares the same interests with Cat. At the top of the remaining columns, write the names of the other animals that want to be Cat's best friend; then list why each animal is not the right kind of best friend for Cat. Your youngsters are sure to learn from Cat that a true best friend is someone to treasure.

George and Martha

Capture the true meaning of friendship by reading this series of stories about the world's two best friends, *George and Martha* by James Marshall (Houghton Mifflin Company). There are many lessons to be learned from these two "hip" friends, so be sure to discuss with youngsters how to apply these lessons in their own friendships. Then follow up with the following song that celebrates friendship.

(sung to the tune of "London Bridge")

[George and Martha] are great friends,
Are great friends, are great friends.
[George and Martha] are great friends.
Hooray for friendship!

Insert the names of other famous friends into the poem, such as Arthur and Buster, Pooh and Piglet, or Mickey and Goofy. Or insert the names of friends from your very own classroom.

My Best Friend

My Best Friend by Pat Hutchins (Greenwillow Books) will help youngsters learn that best friends have their own special gifts to offer one another. After reading the book, discuss how each character has her own unique strengths that make her a good friend. Then give your little ones the opportunity to share their strengths with a friend. Pair each child with a friend. Then encourage each child in a pair of friends to show what she can do well in the classroom, such as build with blocks, complete a puzzle, or draw. When each child has shared her talents with her partner, invite all the children to form one large circle. Ask each child to complete the following sentence: "My friend, [child's name], is really good at _____." That's exactly what good friends do well—make one another feel great!

My friend Nick is really good at singing songs.

The Five Senses

I see with my `ojos`.

I hear with my `orejas`.

I smell with my `nariz`.

I touch with my `manos`.

I taste with my `lengua`.

Spanish Makes Sense to Me

Introduce some Spanish into your five-senses unit to delight and tickle the tongues of your little ones. To begin, write the sentences below on chart paper. Write each Spanish word (shown in parentheses) on a separate sentence strip; then trim each strip so that it fits over the corresponding English word in the chart-paper sentence. For several days, read the sentences in English with your class until they become familiar to youngsters. Then tape each Spanish word over its corresponding English word. Read the sentences with the class again, this time with the Spanish substitutions. Continue to read the sentences together over time. Before long these Spanish words will become natural in your youngsters' vocabulary.

I see with my [eyes].   (ojos)
I hear with my [ears].   (orejas)
I smell with my [nose].   (nariz)
I touch with my [hands].   (manos)
I taste with my [tongue].   (lengua)

Mystery Letters

Get in touch with this sensory approach to letter identification! To prepare, obtain a set of alphabet flash cards. Divide the class into pairs; then have the partners sit pretzel-style, one behind the other. (Make sure all the children are facing you.) Designate the front partner in each pair as the guesser and the back one as the writer. Ask the guessers to lower their heads and cover their eyes while you show the writers a letter card. Lower the card; then invite the guessers to open their eyes. Have each writer use her finger to write the letter from the card on the guesser's back. Then have the guesser whisper to the writer the letter she felt. Encourage the pair to repeat this procedure until the guesser identifies the mystery letter. When all the guessers have determined the letter, have the partners switch roles and repeat the game using a different letter card.

I think that's a B!

Activity	👁	〰	👃	👄	✋
walking on the beach	X	X	X		X
listening to a story	X	X			
eating a meal	X	X	X	X	X
walking through a flower garden	X	X	X		X
taking a bath	X	X	X		X

Senses Journals

If your older students use daily journals, try this activity to explore the five senses. Each day write "see," "taste," "hear," "smell," or "feel" on the chalkboard. Draw a simple body part to symbolize the sense for the day, such as an eye for sight or a nose for smell. Read the word together; then have students draw pictures of things to represent that sense, such as a flower for smell or a radio for hearing. Ask the child to write/dictate a related statement about his illustration on his journal page.

Adapt this activity for younger children by making five-senses books. To make one, staple five sheets of construction paper together. On each page write "Things I can ___." Complete each sentence with a drawing of a body part representing one of the five senses. Help each child cut out magazine pictures related to the sense for the day. Have him glue the cutouts onto the corresponding page; then invite him to share his work with the class.

Team Senses

Do your little ones know that their five senses work together as one team? To demonstrate, give each child an apple slice. Have students eat their apples. Then encourage them to discuss which of their senses helped them to enjoy their apples. Did they see, hear, smell, taste, and feel their apples during this experience? Once youngsters understand that their senses work as a team, complete a chart like the one shown. Include in the first column activities, such as walking on the beach or eating a meal. Then discuss which senses work together as a person performs each activity. Have a volunteer mark each appropriate column on the chart. After completing the chart, review the class findings with students. Which activities work all of our senses at the same time? Which of the five senses is used the most in the listed activities? The least? Look! Listen! Youngsters are working as a team to learn about their teamed-up senses!

Sorting Senses

Use this classification activity to build vocabulary skills around the five senses. To prepare, label each of five envelopes with a different sense; then draw a picture symbol for each one. On each of several notecards, write a descriptive word related to one of the senses, such as *sweet* (taste or smell), *hot* (touch), *loud* (sound), or *bright* (sight).

During group time, lay the envelopes in front of your youngsters. Read the word on a notecard; then ask students to name something that fits the descriptive word. For example, they might respond with "candy" when you read the word *sweet*. Next have a volunteer identify the sense related to the word. (There may be more than one correct answer for some words. Invite youngsters to explain their thinking.) Have him place the card in the corresponding envelope. Continue in this manner until each card is in a "sense-ible" envelope.

The Five Senses

Construction "Sight"

Building observation skills is a snap with this block center idea. In advance, construct three simple structures using an assortment of blocks. Take an instant photo of each structure. Then take each structure apart and put each set of blocks in a separate box. Tape each photo to the box with the corresponding blocks. Have a child in this center select one of the boxes. After he studies the picture, ask him to reproduce the structure in the photo. Then invite him to exchange boxes with a fellow architect until he has had the opportunity to build each of the three structures. This is a true skill-building activity!

name	cookie	pickle	pretzel	chocolate
Georgia	☺	☹	☺	☹
Luke	☺	☹	☺	☹
Anthony	☺	☹	☺	☹
Caroline	☺	☺	☹	☺
Danielle	☺	☹	☹	☹
Charles	☺	☹	☺	☹
Frankie	☺	☺	☹	☹
Christine	☺	☺	☺	☺
Jamie	☺	☺	☺	

Tantalizing Taste Tests

Put your little ones' taste buds to the test at your discovery center. To prepare, list your students' names along the left side of a sheet of chart paper. Then create four columns to the right of the list. At the top of each column, draw a cookie, a pickle, a pretzel, or a square of unsweetened chocolate; then hang the chart in your discovery center. Provide samples of each of the foods on separate plates. Then invite each student to the center to taste each food. After he samples the food, have him mark his taste preferences on the chart by drawing a happy or sad face in the corresponding columns next to his name. Later, as a class, count the number of smiles and frowns to discover which foods passed—or failed—the taste test; then discuss the terms *sweet, sour, salty,* and *bitter*.

Invite your little ones to use their sense of smell in the writing center, of all places! In advance, douse a few cotton balls with a distinctive scent, such as lemon or peppermint extract. Prepare several sets of cotton balls—each with a different scent—and allow all of them to dry. For each scent, label the front of a separate envelope with the scent's name and a picture clue. Then place each set of scented cotton balls in its corresponding envelope.

As each child visits this center, she chooses one envelope at a time. She sniffs the scent, then looks at the label and picture clue. She then draws a picture of what she smelled and, if capable, copies the name of the item onto her own paper.

Polar Bear Club

Invite youngsters to your water table to discover animals belonging to the Polar Bear Club—those that live and play in the waters of the Arctic. To begin, add a bucket of ice cubes to your water table. Then add an assortment of plastic or rubber Arctic animals, such as polar bears, seals, and walruses. Invite your little explorers to play with the animals in the water. Encourage them to talk about the water's temperature and how life might be for the animals that live in and near such cold waters. For an added touch, teach youngsters this chant. Invite them to replace the underlined words with a different Arctic animal name each time they repeat the chant. Welcome to the Polar Br-r-r Club!

[Polar bear, polar bear], will you swim today?
The water's nice and cold. Hurray! Hurray!

What Made That Sound?

Help fine-tune your little ones' sense of hearing as they play this category game at the listening center. To prepare, make a tape of different animal and people sounds with ample pauses programmed between each sound. (You might record animal sounds such as a duck quacking, a dog barking, and a pig snorting, and your recorded people sounds might include laughing, crying, and sneezing.) Then divide a sheet of paper into two columns. Draw an animal at the top of one column and a person at the top of the other. Duplicate a copy for each child; then place the copies in the listening center along with the tape. As each youngster listens to the tape, encourage her to mark the appropriate column for each sound she hears—animal or person. Then have her compare her results with another child's. Shhh. Listen. What made that sound?

119

The Five Senses

Sailing the Deep "See"

Make youngsters aware of their amazing sense of sight with this "deep-see" activity. In advance prepare a large batch of blue gelatin in a clear glass or plastic bowl. Cut a variety of alphabet letters (ones your students can identify) from blue construction paper. Place the letters in an envelope; then set the bowl of set gelatin and the envelope on the floor in your circle area. Explain that each child will have a turn to look into the deep blue sea (the gelatin) to see if she can see anything at the bottom.

Slip a letter beneath the bowl. Then teach youngsters this song:

Some Children Went to Sea
(sung to the tune of "A Sailor Went to Sea")

Some children went to sea-sea-sea
To see what they could see-see-see.
They saw the letter [R - R - R]
At the bottom of the deep sea-sea-sea!

Invite a few children to gather around the bowl and see what they can see at the bottom of the sea. Once they have correctly identified the letter, sing the song, inserting the name of the letter into the third line. Repeat the activity until every child has had a turn to "see-see-see" a letter.

Touch and Go

Don't pass up this activity that explores the sense of touch. To prepare, gather several items with interesting textures, such as a tennis ball, a small stuffed animal, or a shell. Put one item in a large grocery bag and fold the top over. At circle time, have youngsters pass the bag as you sing the following song:

Pass, Pass, Pass the Bag
(sung to the tune of "Row, Row, Row Your Boat")

Pass, pass, pass the bag,
Round and round it goes.
What could be inside it now?
What do you suppose?

When you stop singing, have the child holding the bag reach inside to feel and guess its contents. Remind the child not to peek! After he announces his guess, have the next child in the circle display the item for all to see. Repeat this touch-and-go game with additional items.

Now Hear This!

Your students are bound to shout, "Hear! Hear!" to this listening activity! In advance tape-record each child speaking. Ask each youngster to repeat a specified sentence, or record the children's candid conversations throughout the course of a day. In the days that follow, play the tape to see if the children can identify their own voices and those of their classmates. What an earful of fun!

Colorful Cuisine

Add a little color to your study of the five senses with this taste test. In advance add enough red food coloring to a half-gallon of milk to tint it pink; then pour a small cup of pink milk for each child. Next mix cream cheese with blue food coloring and spread it on a minibagel for each child. Display the bagels and milk during circle time, and tell your youngsters they will be invited to try these treats during snacktime. Ask them if they think they will like the taste of the pink milk and blue cream cheese; then chart their responses. After snack, record their responses to these colorful culinary treats. Did their reactions match their predictions?

A "Scent-sible" Match

"Odor" up some fun with this matching game. To prepare, program a card for each child with a smiley face on one side and a frowning face on the other. Next cut three bottle shapes from construction paper. Gather three fragrant items, such as cinnamon, orange extract, and cocoa powder. Rub a different fragrance onto each paper bottle to transfer the scent. Then put some cinnamon, a few orange wedges, and a chocolate candy bar in separate lunch bags. During circle time, distribute the programmed cards. Pass one paper bottle for all students to smell. Then pass one lunch bag. Ask your youngsters to determine whether or not the scent in the bag matches the scent on the bottle. If they decide the scents match, have them hold their cards with the smiley faces toward you. If they decide the scents are different, have them display the frowning sides of their cards. Continue the game until each scent has met its match. Then reveal each bag's contents.

The Five Senses

Cool Paintings

Invite your little artists to experience a cool way to paint. To make cool paintbrushes, insert a craft stick into a small, water-filled paper cup for each child; then freeze the cups overnight. Set up your art center with the cups of ice, construction paper, plastic spoons, and powdered tempera paint in assorted colors. Invite each child at this center to sprinkle a spoonful of each paint color onto her paper. Then have her peel the paper cup away from her ice-cube paintbrush. Encourage her to rub her frozen paintbrush through the dry paint and all over her paper. As the ice melts and spreads the paint colors on her paper, she will delight in watching a cool painting appear before her eyes! Once the paint dries, invite each child to use markers to add details to her nice ice painting.

Sounds of the Kitchen

Cook up some fun from the kitchen while giving youngsters some sound finger exercise. Gather from the kitchen a rolling pin, a cutting board, a nut chopper, a handheld can opener, an eggbeater, and a bowl. Set up the utensils on a classroom table. Put the eggbeater in a bowl of water, the rolling pin on the cutting board, and shelled walnuts in the nut chopper. Then attach the can opener to an unopened can. Discuss the name and function of each utensil with the class. Then hold a bedsheet or a length of bulletin-board paper in front of the table. Invite a volunteer to manipulate a utensil of his choice behind the sheet. Challenge the class to guess the kitchen instrument being used by listening to the sound it makes. Then invite all the students to pantomime using the instrument themselves. After they've guessed the first one, continue making more kitchen music.

A Fruity "Sense-sation"

Things are sure to get juicy when your youngsters try this fruity fine-motor activity. Give each child a tangerine or an orange. Have him hold the fruit in his hands to feel its shape, texture, and firmness. Invite him to smell the fruit and comment on its scent. Demonstrate how to peel the skin; then invite each child to peel his own fruit. (Assist younger children as necessary.) As he removes the peel, ask him to notice whether or not the fruit's scent becomes stronger. Are his taste buds tingling as he smells the scent? Once the fruit is peeled, have each child pull apart the segments of his fruit. Ask him to hold his largest segment up to the light. Have him watch for a spray of fruit-juice as he pulls both ends of the segment back at the same time. (The spray comes from broken juice sacs inside the fruit.) Did he hear the sound of the spray? Ask the child to release the spray from the remaining sections of his fruit. Then invite him to do one last "sense-ible" thing—sink his teeth into this sensational fruit!

Symphony of Sounds

These shakers are a sound way to orchestrate some fine-motor activity. Collect a class supply of small, lidded baby-food jars and an assortment of noisemaking items such as dried pasta, pennies, jingle bells, wooden beads, and sand. (Make certain the sound of each item can be discriminated from the others.) Cut a piece of gift wrap in which to wrap each jar. You'll also need some tongs, tweezers, scoops, tape, and curling ribbon.

Invite each child in a small group to create a shaker. To make one, a child uses tongs, tweezers, or a scoop to partially fill a jar with her choice of material; then she screws the lid onto the jar. She wraps the jar in a piece of paper, tying the excess paper at the top of the jar with a length of curling ribbon. Once all your groups have made their shakers, invite the children to take turns shaking them. Challenge the class to guess which item is inside each shaker. Then group together youngsters with same-sound shakers to conduct the class in a symphony of sounds.

Pudding Picasso

Tempt each of your little artists to produce a tasty work of art. In advance, purchase a class supply of quart-sized resealable plastic bags, milk, and a few boxes of instant pudding in varied flavors. (Be sure to select flavors that will produce different colors.) From each plastic bag, snip one bottom corner to create a small hole. Mix separate batches of pudding; then place each container of pudding on a table, along with the bags and a supply of plastic spoons and plates.

Working with one small group at a time, have each child spoon some pudding into a plastic bag and then seal it. Encourage the child to squeeze the pudding through the hole in her bag onto a plastic plate with a decorative flair. Then have her repeat the process, refilling her bag each time with a different pudding color. Finally, encourage the child to create some finger designs on her plate. This art is truly tasty—the proof is in the pudding!

The Five Senses

Sing a Song of Senses

Teach your youngsters this song about our five senses. For added fun, sing the song repeated times, increasing or decreasing the speed as you desire.

We Have Five Senses
(sung to the tune of "Head, Shoulders, Knees, and Toes")

We have five senses, you know.
Yes, we know.
We have five senses, you know.
Yes, we know.
We see, hear, taste, smell,
   and touch.
Our senses help us grow.
Don't you know?

Hold up five fingers.
Nod head "yes."
Hold up five fingers.
Nod head "yes."
Point to eyes, ears, mouth,
   nose, and fingers.
Stretch arms overhead.

The Sound of Silence

Work those senses! Ask your little ones to stand far apart from one another. Stand in front of your youngsters; then lead them in a series of exercises, such as circling arms, lifting knees, marching, jumping, and twisting from side to side. In your verbal commands, include the number of times the students should do each exercise. Then direct students to watch you carefully as you repeat the series of exercises without speaking. Hold up the appropriate number of fingers to let youngsters know how many times to repeat each exercise. The only sounds in the room should be the pitter-patter of little feet working out!

Skin Deep

Get "touchy-feely" with your youngsters! On a warm day, ask your little ones to take off their footwear. Invite them to walk, run, skip, and jump on different outdoor surfaces, such as grass, concrete, dirt, sand, and blacktop. How do the various surfaces feel on their feet? Take the students indoors to experience other textures. Provide textured items, such as cotton, satin, sandpaper, and metal. Encourage your little ones to rub these textured items on their hands, arms, or legs. Anywhere there is skin, there is the sense of touch. It's a touchy subject children just love to explore!

What Scent Was Sent?

Youngsters will quickly catch on to this guessing game. Prepare a small paper lunch bag for each child by punching holes in the top with a hole puncher. Put one of the following inside each bag: a piece of chocolate, an orange slice, a mint candy, or any food with a recognizable scent. Staple all the bags shut and put them in a basket near the slide on your playground. Gather your little ones around the slide. Take a bag and climb the ladder. Select a child to catch the bag; then slide it down to her. Ask the child to sniff the bag and guess the contents; then invite her to open the bag and view what's inside. Have her take a new bag, climb the ladder, and send the bag down the slide to another child. After everyone has had a turn to both catch and slide, invite youngsters to use their sense of taste to enjoy a "scent-sational" treat, such as orange wedges.

Out of Sight

Help your little ones understand what it is like to be without the sense of sight. Place a jump rope on the ground for your students to take turns walking on. (Use two jump ropes if you would like to minimize waiting time.) Encourage youngsters to walk at a comfortable pace while maintaining their balance. Then divide your class into pairs. Ask youngsters to walk the jump rope a second time, but with their eyes closed. Have each partner take turns offering a guiding hand to the "sightless" child.

The Five Senses

Five Senses Sipper

Ingredients:
approximately 1/2 cup orange juice per child
approximately 1/4 cup seltzer per child
2 ice cubes per child
1 orange slice per child

Utensils and Supplies:
one 8-ounce plastic cup per child
2 small pitchers
knife

Teacher Preparation:
Cut the oranges into slices. On each slice, cut along one section line from the rind to the center. Pour the orange juice and seltzer into separate pitchers.
Arrange the ingredients and utensils near the step-by-step direction cards.

What to Do When the Snack Is Through

Here is a "sense-ible" and scientific way to use your leftover ingredients. Put the following into three separate jars: 1/4 cup orange juice, 1/4 cup seltzer, and two ice cubes. Tightly fasten the lids; then display the jars in front of the class. How are the contents of the jars different? How are they the same? Shake each jar for several seconds; then ask youngsters to describe what they see and hear. Blindfold a student; then shake the jars again. Can she determine the contents of the jars by what she hears? Remove the lids. Can she guess the contents of the jars by what she smells?

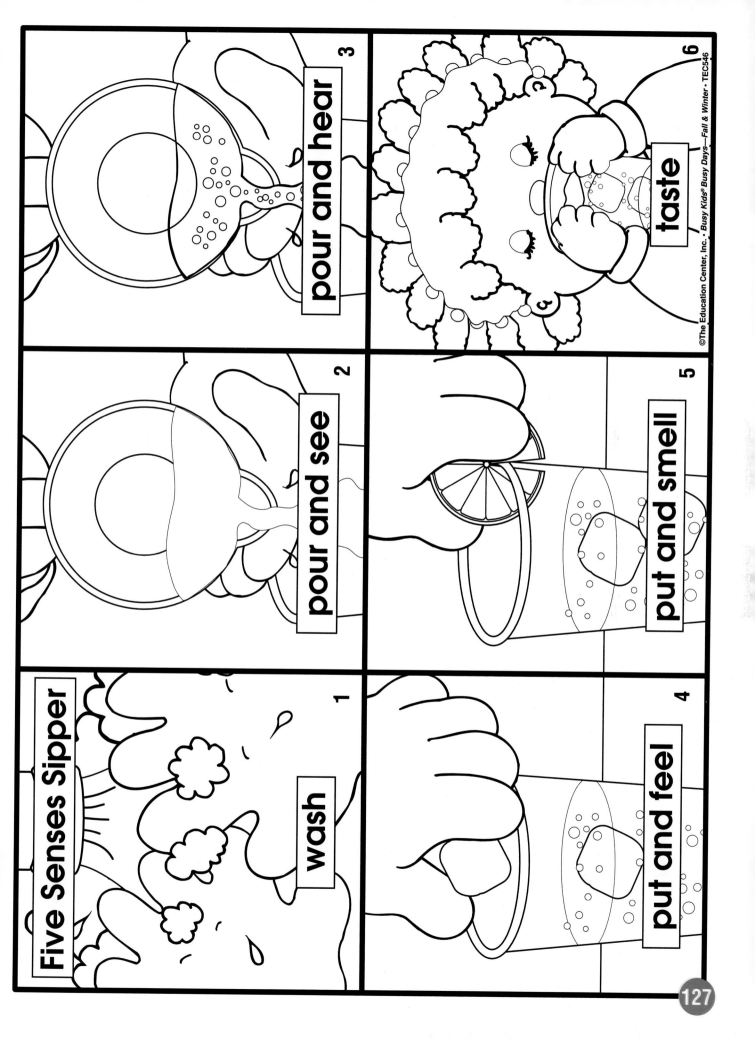

Five Senses Sipper

wash
1

pour and see
2

pour and hear
3

put and feel
4

put and smell
5

taste
6

©The Education Center, Inc. • Busy Kids® Busy Days—Fall & Winter • TEC546

The Five Senses

Discovering My World

*(sung to the tune of
"You Are My Sunshine")*

I have five senses,
Five helpful senses,
Teaching me all things
I want to know.
I use my eyes, ears,
Mouth, nose, and fingers
To discover the world as I grow!

Can You Hear This?

Before singing this tune, gather a few items you can use to make noises, such as a bell, a pair of sand blocks, a toy drum, and a pair of scissors. Place the items in a bag or basket. Sing the verse once; then ask the child whose name you sang in the third and fourth lines to turn his back to the group. Remove one of the items from the bag or basket and use it to make a noise. Ask the child to identify the item from its sound. Then continue with other verses, giving other students turns to test their sense of hearing.

*(sung to the tune of
"Are You Sleeping?")*

Are you listening,
Are you listening,
My friend [child's name]?
My friend [child's name]?
Hearing is a sense
That is magnificent!
Don't you agree?
Don't you agree?

Senses Work in Harmony

(sung to the tune of "Twinkle, Twinkle, Little Star")

My senses are a part of me—
A nose to smell and eyes to see,
Ears to hear and hands to touch,
A tongue to taste good food and
     such.
My senses are a part of me,
Working all in harmony.

I Do!

Teach youngsters this happy song about their senses. Once they become familiar with the song, challenge students' sensory knowledge and their listening skills by changing the words so that each sense is mismatched with a body part. For example, you might sing, "If you smell with your eyes, say 'I do.'" Encourage youngsters to listen carefully in order give the appropriate response for each line: "I do" or "I don't."

(sung to the tune of "If You're Happy and You Know It")

If you smell with your nose, say "I do."   *Shout "I do!"*
If you see with your eyes, say "I do."   *Shout "I do!"*

If you taste with your tongue
And it makes you say "Yum! Yum!"
If you taste with your tongue, say "I do."   *Shout "I do!"*

If you hear with your ears, say "I do."   *Shout "I do!"*
If you touch with your hands, say "I do."   *Shout "I do!"*

If your senses help you grow,
Teaching all you need to know,
If your senses help you grow, say "They do!"   *Shout "They do!"*

The Five Senses

My Five Senses

Five young children take the reader on a photographic tour of the senses in *My Five Senses* by Margaret Miller (Aladdin Paperbacks). After reading through the book once, turn to the introduction page that features pictures of each of the five children pointing to body parts that go with their senses. Point to the first child's picture and say, "Eyes are for…," inviting the class to complete the sentence with the word *seeing.* Repeat this for each of the five pictures, focusing on the featured body part. Next, open the book to any two-page spread. Ask the children to name the sense that is being used in each photograph. If a clue is needed, provide the corresponding body part. It's a follow-up activity that just makes sense!

Hands are for touching!

Charles

The Story of Ferdinand

The Story of Ferdinand by Munro Leaf (Viking Press) was first published more than 50 years ago and has stood the test of time as generations have enjoyed the simple story of the peaceful bull that would rather smell flowers than fight. After sharing this story with your little ones, set up a smelling center with drawing paper and a combination of scented and unscented markers. Invite individual children to sort the markers into two groups: scented and unscented. If possible, provide two matching sets of scented markers so students can also pair together markers with the same scent. After the child has finished sorting, encourage him to sniff the scented markers and guess the scent of each one. (Be prepared for some colored noses after this activity!) Then encourage your Ferdinand fans to use the scented markers to draw Ferdinand sitting "just quietly" and smelling the flowers.

Popcorn smells ___buttery___.
Popcorn tastes ___salty___.
Popcorn feels ___crunchy___.
Popcorn looks ___white___.
Popcorn sounds ___fast___.

My Five Senses

Aliki's *My Five Senses* (Harper Trophy) helps youngsters understand how we experience things with the help of our senses. After reading the simple text, teach your children the following song to reinforce their knowledge of the senses and their corresponding body parts.

(sung to the tune of "Do You Know the Muffin Man?")

Do you know how I [see] things?
How I [see] things? How I [see] things?
Do you know how I [see] things?
I [see] things with my [eyes].
Point to the body part.

Sing additional verses for the other senses.

You Smell and Taste and Feel and See and Hear

Experience a dog day afternoon through the senses of a delightful dog in *You Smell and Taste and Feel and See and Hear* by Mary Murphy (DK Publishing, Inc.). Then try this extension that will put little ones' five senses to work. Put a bag of microwave popcorn in the microwave (or pour kernels into a hot air popper) without the children seeing. Invite them to close their eyes and listen. As they hear and smell the popcorn popping, have them name the body parts and senses they are using. Can they tell you what is happening? When the popcorn is done popping, show it to the class and invite each child to put a handful of popcorn on a napkin. How does the popcorn look and feel? Now have them enjoy the taste. Next write the phrases shown on your chalkboard and encourage the class to provide the endings.

Another "Sense-ational" Idea

Select any page from *You Smell and Taste and Feel and See and Hear* or a page that features a sensory experience from either of the two *My Five Senses* books and discuss the sense or senses being used in the picture. Then give each child a copy of the reproducible on page 203. Encourage the child to draw a smiley face in each column that shows a sense being used in the illustration. Continue in this manner using other pages from these five-star five-senses books.

Christmas

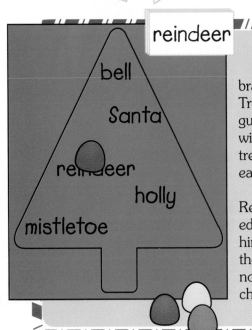

reindeer

bell

Santa

reindeer

holly

mistletoe

Yum-Yum Tree

Oh, Christmas tree! Oh, Christmas tree! How yummy are your branches! That's what youngsters will think when they play Christmas Tree Bingo. To prepare, gather small candies such as holiday M&M's® or gumdrops. Program index cards with Christmas-related words that begin with different consonants. To make gameboards, draw a simple Christmas tree on several sheets of green construction paper. Randomly program each tree with several words corresponding to those on the index cards.

To play, give each child in a small group a gameboard and some candy. Read a word card to the group. Encourage each child to use his knowledge of beginning sounds to try to find that word on his gameboard. Have him mark it with a piece of candy. To check for accuracy, show youngsters the word card. Adapt this game for younger children by programming the notecards and gameboards with matching Christmas stickers. When a child covers his entire tree, invite him to eat his candies. Yum! Yum!

How many days till Christmas?
This chain will help you count.
Cut one candy off each day.
You've got the right amount.

When the candy is all gone,
You ring the bell and say,
"Peace and joy and love to all.
Tomorrow is Christmas Day!"

Christmas Countdown

Help anxious youngsters count down the days until Christmas with this candy chain. To prepare, purchase or ask parents to donate enough individually wrapped candies so that you have seven per child. Seven days before Christmas, have each child place his candies in a row down the middle of a 28-inch length of plastic wrap. Help him wrap his candies in the plastic as shown. Then have him tie a length of curling ribbon around the plastic wrap between each candy and at each end of the chain. Invite the child to tie a jingle bell and a copy of the poem shown onto the ribbon at one end of the chain. Invite children to take their candy countdown chains home or to use them at school, cutting off one piece of candy each day until Christmas.

ABC Garland

Decorate your classroom for the holidays with this alphabet garland. In advance, drape a Christmas garland along a bulletin board, window, or wall. Then write the alphabet down the left side of a sheet of chart paper. Over several days, have your little elves brainstorm Christmas-related words that begin with each letter. List their responses on the chart paper. Once the list is complete, assign one letter to each child. (Invite volunteers to take any leftover letters.) Encourage her to choose a word beginning with her letter from the list and illustrate it on a construction paper circle. On the back of the circle—or ornament—write her dictated description, such as "*C* is for candy cane." Punch a hole in each ornament; then insert an ornament hanger in the hole. Invite students to hang their ornaments in alphabetical order on the garland.

Holiday Card Match

"Ho-ho-hold" onto those used holiday cards to reinforce sorting and beginning sounds. Collect a variety of cards with simple holiday pictures (preferably with only one item on the front, such as a bell or a reindeer). Cut off the card fronts; then label each one with the beginning letter and the word shown in the picture. Help your students identify each picture and letter. Then place the cards in a center. Invite a child to sort them, either by similar pictures or by matching beginning sounds.

Jingle All the Way

Youngsters love to sing "Jingle Bells" at Christmastime. So they're sure to love this read-along sing-along using their own jingle-bell pointers. In advance, write the song's chorus on chart paper. Then write each word of the chorus on a separate sentence strip length. Back each strip with magnetic tape. To make a pointer, each child folds a pipe cleaner in half. He strings three small jingle bells down to the fold and then twists together the free ends of the pipe cleaner. Then he inserts the twisted pipe cleaner snugly into a skinny straw until only the bells show. To use the pointer, each child, in turn, leads the class in singing the song, using his pointer to point to each word. When each student masters the one-to-one correspondence of spoken to written words, challenge him to sequence the word strips on a magnetic board. (Display the chart paper song as a reference.) Your little ones will be jingling all the way to beginning reading!

Christmas

Season's Readings

Book time for plenty of Christmas reading this season. After reading an assortment of Christmas books to your little ones, display three of the books on a table in your reading center. Ask each child to illustrate the Christmas story he most enjoyed. Label his drawing with the title of the book. Then display each child's illustration with the corresponding title. Which book is the class favorite? Whatever the results, season's readings abound!

Rodney

Rudolph, the Red-Nosed Reindeer

Stocking Sense

Heighten the senses of the season at your discovery center. To prepare, wrap three small items in holiday gift wrap and place them inside a large Christmas stocking. On a sheet of chart paper, draw the three items along with three more items that are not inside the stocking; then hang the chart paper near the stocking.

Ask each child who visits this center to use her senses of touch, sight, hearing, and even smell to guess what the three objects are. Have her indicate her guess by putting a check beside the drawings that represent her guesses. At the end of the day, discuss the children's guesses; then unwrap the three packages for all to see. Repeat the activity on another day by wrapping three different items to put inside the stocking.

What Is in the Stocking?

paper clip
block ✔✔
paintbrush
jingle bells ✔✔✔
Hershey's® Kisses® ✔✔
book ✔

Seasonal Gift Wrap

Wrap up the Christmas season with this art-center activity. Stock your art center with a variety of Christmas cookie cutters, 12-inch lengths of white bulletin-board paper (one for each child), and shallow trays of red and green tempera paint. Invite the children to make cookie-cutter prints on their papers. Encourage them to experiment with various designs, colors, and patterns as they work. After the paint dries, allow each student to use her decorated paper to wrap a special gift for a special someone.

Ornamental Math

Shape up your math table for the holidays with this festive sorting activity. In advance, send each child home with a note requesting that he bring an unbreakable Christmas ornament to school. Then cut out one small, one medium, and one large construction-paper circle. Place a small artificial tree and the cutouts in the math center. As children bring their ornaments to school, have them hang their decorations on the tree. When the tree is fully decorated, encourage small groups of youngsters to remove the ornaments and place each one on the construction-paper circle corresponding to its size (small, medium, or large). After all the ornaments have been sorted, invite your little elves to trim the tree all over again!

Santa Station

Convert your dramatic-play center into a Santa station. Gather items to create a Santa costume, such as a Santa hat, a white beard, an oversized red shirt, black boots, and a large sack (or a pillowcase). Collect more Santa hats and long red shirts to serve as elf costumes. Wrap several small boxes or cardboard blocks in holiday paper; then place them in the center along with the Santa props and a tape recording of holiday music. Hang several stockings on a wall or table in the center. Then invite youngsters to use the props to role-play Santa and his elves preparing for the big event. Ho! Ho! Ho!

Susan Hodnett

Christmas

The Sounds of Christmas

Ring in the holiday with a jingling review of Christmas sounds. To prepare, put several jingle bells inside a clean, empty potato-chip canister. Secure the lid; then wrap the canister with some holiday paper. Have the children sit in a circle; then roll the canister to one student as you recite the following verse:

Jingle bells, jingle bells, roll around.
Can you name a Christmas sound?

Ask the child who receives the canister to name a sound associated with Christmas, such as sleigh bells ringing, a fireplace crackling, or Santa saying, "Ho, ho, ho." Then have him roll the canister to someone else. The recipient repeats the sound named by the previous child, then names a Christmas sound of his own. Continue until there are no more sounds to go around!

Jingle bells, jingle bells...

Reindeer!

The Sights of Christmas

Your youngsters will gain a little "insight" into vocabulary with this holiday idea. Prepare a set of holiday cards by cutting pictures from old Christmas cards featuring holiday designs such as ornaments, poinsettias, or Christmas trees. If desired, include symbols associated with multicultural holidays such as Hanukkah and Kwanzaa. Mount each picture on an index card; then distribute one card to each child. Provide clues to describe one of the holiday pictures. Encourage the child whose picture matches the description to hold up his card for all to see. Name—or have the child name—the picture on his card. Then continue to describe the sights of the season.

Mmm, chocolate!

The Smells of Christmas

Have your youngsters take a whiff of this "scent-sational" activity to heighten the senses. In advance place enough Hershey's® Kisses® or mini candy canes for each child inside a box; then wrap the box in holiday paper. Carefully make several small slits in the box to allow the fragrance to filter through. Have your youngsters sit in a circle; then pass the box to a child. Ask him to smell it, think about what might be inside, and then pass it to the next child. After everyone has had a chance to smell the box, ask children to guess the contents. Record their responses; then open the box to see if anyone guessed correctly.

The Touch of Christmas

Christmas is full of surprises, and so is a game of Santa's Secret Sack. In advance select a few Christmas-related items of different shapes, such as a wrapped candy cane, a small wreath and a non-breakable ornament. Put one of the items in a large pillowcase (without youngsters seeing the item). Then don a Santa hat and recite the following poem. Once everyone has had a turn to reach into the bag, ask the class to identify the contents of the pillowcase. Continue the game with the remaining items.

What's inside Santa's sack?
Reach right in and touch.
Can you tell what it might be?
Do you have a hunch?

The Shapes of Christmas

Watch math concepts shape up with a holiday flannelboard. Cut from felt a large green triangle, a yellow star, a brown rectangle, small colorful circles and ovals, and various sizes of squares and rectangles. Distribute the felt cutouts randomly. Have the children identify the various felt shapes; then challenge them to work together to make a Christmas picture using all of the felt cutouts. You may be surprised by what takes shape!

Christmas

3-D Trees

Fine-motor practice is a real "tree-t" with this activity! To prepare, cut a few tree shapes (similar to the one shown) from tagboard. For each child, fold a 9" x 12" sheet of green construction paper into thirds. Set up a center with the folded paper, the tagboard tree patterns, pencils, sticky dots, scissors, and glue. To make a three-dimensional tree, a child traces a tree pattern onto folded green construction paper, and then cuts it out through all thicknesses of the paper. He folds the stack of three trees in half lengthwise. Then he glues the three trees together (as shown, with the folds in the center) to make a three-dimensional tree. For a finishing touch, he decorates his 3-D tree with sticky-dot "ornaments."

A Pocket Full of Christmas Cheer

Sharpen your students' sewing skills when they lace up these festive Christmas pockets. To prepare, gather two recycled Christmas cards of similar size for each child. Cut the fronts off of each card in a pair; then discard the backs. Trim the cards so that they are identical in size. Holding the cards together back-to-back, punch holes around three sides. Thread one end of a yarn length through a hole in one top corner; then tie it in place. Wrap a piece of tape around the other end of the yarn to make lacing easier.

Invite each child to lace the yarn through a prepared card pair; then help him tie the yarn in place at the last hole. String another length of yarn through the top holes of the resulting pocket to create a handle. Collect the pockets; then secretly insert into each one a small Christmas treat, such as a sticker or a mini candy cane. Later, present these pockets full of Christmas cheer to your youngsters as a fun surprise.

Candy Cane Creations

Sweeten patterning and fine-motor skills with these beaded candy canes. To begin, cut a six-inch length of a red or white pipe cleaner for each child. Then give each child a supply of red and white beads. (It will take approximately 25 pony beads to complete one candy cane.) Show him how to bend one end of his pipe cleaner into a loop to keep the beads from falling off. Then direct him to thread the beads onto the pipe cleaner in an alternating red and white pattern. When the last bead is threaded, help the child loop the other end of the pipe cleaner to secure the beads. Then have him bend the pipe cleaner to resemble a candy cane. Encourage youngsters to brighten their homes with these handmade ornaments.

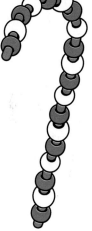

Fingerpaint With Pizzazz

Encourage your little elves to add a "scent-sational" sparkle to their fingerpaintings this holiday season. To prepare scented paint, add peppermint flavoring to your red or green fingerpaint. Then invite youngsters to use the paint to create seasonal paintings. While the paint is still wet, have little ones sprinkle red, green, or silver glitter onto their creations. Not only will these aromatic paintings sparkle, but so will your students' smiles as they admire their holiday art!

Wraparound Wreath

Wrap up some holiday smiles with these irresistible wreaths. In advance, gather a few toilet-paper tubes and a supply of red and white pipe cleaners. Cut the tubes in half; then cut a slit in one end of each tube half. Cut the pipe cleaners into enough two-inch lengths for each child to have four to six pieces. Then cut a three-yard length of green yarn for each child. Ask a small group to watch as you demonstrate how to make a wreath with the materials. Then help the children make their own wreaths.

To make a wreath, slip one end of the yarn into the tube slit. Wrap the yarn around the tube to cover it. Then trap the loose end under the wrapped yarn. Pinch the yarn together in one spot; then slip a pipe-cleaner piece under the gathers. Wrap the pipe cleaner around the yarn; then slip the yarn circle off the tube. Wrap a few more pipe-cleaner pieces around the wreath in various spots, securing the loose ends of the yarn and defining the wreath's shape. It's a wreath, and...that's a wrap!

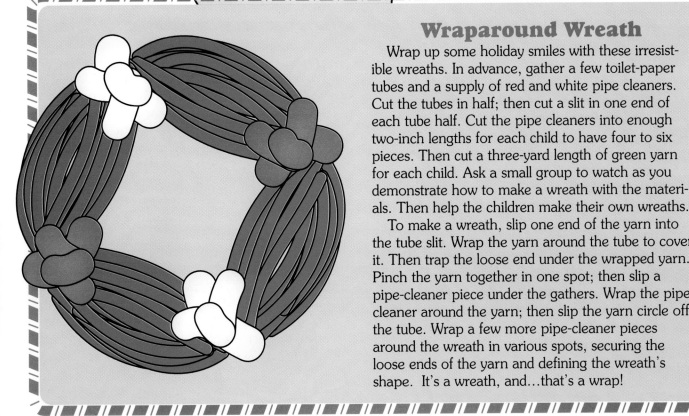

Christmas

Catch the Christmas Spirit

Help your little ones catch the Christmas spirit with this catching game. In advance, inflate enough large round balloons for half of the class. Using a permanent marker, draw one of the following on each balloon to represent the concepts of *peace, love,* and *giving:* two people holding hands, a big heart, and a gift in extended hands. In a large group, discuss the meanings of peace, love, and giving in relation to Christmas. Then divide the class into partners and give each pair a balloon. Have the partners stand a few feet apart and toss the balloon back and forth to each other. Can they toss the balloon high? Low? Fast? Slow? For an added challenge, have partners stand farther apart with each toss. When the game is over, all your youngsters will have caught the Christmas spirit!

Christmas Jingling

Your youngsters will be jingling as they go a-caroling along! Prepare a jingle bracelet for each child by threading a pipe cleaner through two jingle bells, then twisting the ends of the pipe cleaner together. Give a jingle bracelet to each child to wear on his wrist. Have youngsters shake their bells to the rhythm as they sing "Jingle Bells" and "We Wish You a Merry Christmas." For added fun, have each student put his bracelet around his ankle and shake a leg!

After some practice, take your Christmas show on the road. March your jolly jinglers to other classrooms, and treat each audience to a holiday song.

Santa Says

Help Santa and his elves keep fit for the Christmas season with this holiday version of Simon Says. Form a circle with your little ones; then select one child to be Santa. Have Santa demonstrate an action that he wants his elves—the class—to repeat. Suggest actions such as hopping on one foot, running in place, or touching toes. After the elves follow Santa's lead, choose another child to take over as Santa. The game continues until everyone in the circle has had a turn being jolly old Saint Nick.

Rudolph, the Flying Reindeer

Imaginations will take flight as your little reindeer fly along with Rudolph. Encourage youngsters to respond to the following song with corresponding movements. In repeated verses, substitute other action words for "flying," such as *hopping, galloping, prancing,* and *leaping.*

Rudolph, the Flying Reindeer

(sung to the tune of "Rudolph, the Red-Nosed Reindeer")

Rudolph, the [flying] reindeer,
Loved to [fly] all day and night.
And if you ever saw him,
You'd agree it was a sight!

The Circle of Giving

Play this circle game to help show your little ones that giving is as important as receiving. In advance, wrap one small (inexpensive) treat for each child in holiday paper. Then put the treats in a large basket. Invite your little ones to form a circle. With seasonal music playing, have the students pass the basket around the circle. When the music stops, invite the youngster holding the basket to skip around the circle to another child and offer him a gift from the basket. Encourage the recipient to say, "Thank you." Continue the game until every child has received a present. Wrap things up by inviting each child to open his gift.

141

Christmas

Christmas Angel

Ingredients:
1 slice of angel food cake per child
1 vanilla wafer per child
tubes of red and green decorating icing
1 Gummi Savers® candy per child

Utensils and Supplies:
knife
napkins

Teacher Preparation:
Cut each slice of angel food cake in half diagonally. Then cut one of the halves on the diagonal again, to give each child a total of three triangles. Arrange the ingredients and utensils near the step-by-step direction cards.

What to Do When the Snack Is Through

After youngsters make a yummy Christmas snack for themselves, invite them to make one for their feathered friends. Give each child two leftover vanilla wafers, peanut butter, and a pipe cleaner. Instruct each child to spread peanut butter on the bottoms of both cookies, then stick them together. Help him loop the pipe cleaner around the cookies and twist the ends together. Have him bend the twisted pipe cleaner into a hook shape. Have him spread more peanut butter over the outside of his cookie ornament, then dip it in birdseed. Hang the finished cookie ornaments on a tree for the birds to eat.

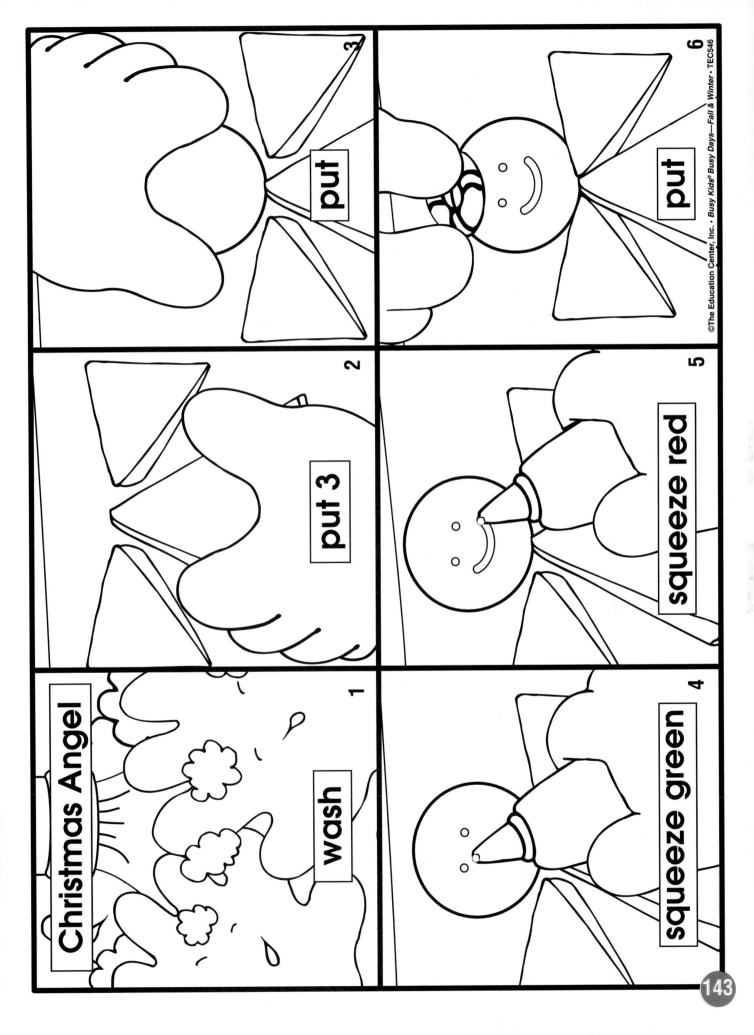

©The Education Center, Inc. • Busy Kids® Busy Days—Fall & Winter • TEC546

Christmas

Beneath My Christmas Tree

Ring in the holiday season with this jolly jingle. To make a jingle bell to use with the song, have each youngster thread a bell onto a pipe cleaner and then twist the ends together.

(sung to the tune of "Jingle Bells")

Santa Claus,	*Ring bell.*
Santa Claus,	*Ring bell.*
Won't you lend an ear?	*Hold hand up to ear.*
I have been so very good	*Pat shoulder.*
All throughout the year.	*Extend arms out to sides.*
Santa Claus,	*Ring bell.*
Santa Claus,	*Ring bell.*
Wouldn't you agree?	*Shake head up and down.*
I deserve a special treat	*Point to self.*
Beneath my Christmas tree!	*Make triangle with hands.*

Twinkle Little Lights

Brighten things up with this song about Christmas lights. Have youngsters stand in a circle. Then encourage them to dance to the song as they point and bend their fingers to represent shimmering lights.

(sung to the tune of "Twinkle, Twinkle, Little Star")

Twinkle, twinkle, little lights,
Winking, blinking through the night.
Lighting up my Christmas tree,
Twinkling oh-so-merrily.
Twinkle, twinkle, little lights,
What a bright and awesome sight!

My Favorite Time of Year

(sung to the tune of "Dreidel, Dreidel, Dreidel")

Christmas, Christmas, Christmas,
My favorite time of year.
Christmas, Christmas, Christmas,
It's full of love and cheer.

Christmas, Christmas, Christmas,
It fills me with such glee.
Christmas, Christmas, Christmas,
It's Christmas Day! Yippee!

Joy to All

(sung to the tune of "Row, Row, Row Your Boat")

Joy, joy, joy to all,
Christmas time is here!
Love fills our hearts right from the start,
At this time of year.

Joy, joy, joy to all,
Christmas time is here!
A time to give, a time to live,
A time to give a cheer!

I'm a Little Present

As anticipation for the big day builds, build up students' inference skills with this peekaboo-present idea. Wrap the top and bottom of a gift box separately in holiday paper. Each day, secretly put a different Christmas-related item—such as a candy cane, an ornament, or a stocking—inside the box. Then, during group time, have students pass the present around the circle while you sing this song. When the song ends, have the child holding the box peek inside it. Encourage him to provide clues about the item, without revealing its identity, while the class tries to guess what it is.

(sung to the tune of "I'm a Little Teapot")

I'm a little present
Just for you,
Because you are special—
Yes, it's true.

Please don't open me till
Christmas Day.
Oh! I can't wait—
Take a peek today!

This is something shiny!

145

Christmas

Elephant and Mouse Get Ready for Christmas

Learn lessons about friendship from a big-hearted friend in *Elephant and Mouse Get Ready for Christmas* by Lois G. Grambling (Barron's Educational Series, Inc.). To prepare for this extension activity, gather and label a large stocking for Mouse and a small stocking for Elephant. Collect a class supply of small toys from your classroom, being sure to include a few toys that are small enough to fit inside the small stocking. As you read the story, pause immediately after Elephant switches the names on the stockings. To help children understand Elephant's act of kindness, lay the stockings on the floor in front of the class and distribute the toys to the children. Ask one child at a time to place his toy inside a stocking. Once all the toys are delivered, ask youngsters to tell you which stocking is holding more gifts. Count to confirm their answer. Ask them to explain why they think Elephant switched the names on the stockings. Encourage predictions about the outcome of this delightful story before you read on.

Only a Star

Programs that celebrate the religious aspect of Christmas will enjoy the story of the first Christmas as told in *Only a Star* by Margery Facklam (William B. Eerdmans Publishing Company, Inc.). Ask youngsters to identify the baby on the cover of the book. Ask student volunteers to describe the story of the first Christmas as they know it. Then read the story to your youngsters, telling them of the star that turns the simplest objects into glistening decorations to welcome baby Jesus. As an extension, invite each child to make a manger scene. Give each child a set

of nativity stickers. (These are available at teacher stores or Christian bookstores. If you can't find them, cut out pictures of Mary, Joseph, and Jesus from used Christmas cards.) To make a manger scene, the child glues four craft sticks in the shape of a manger to a sheet of construction paper. Then she glues (or sticks) the characters inside the manger. Squeeze glue in the shape of a star in the upper corner of the child's nativity scene. Then have her sprinkle gold glitter on top of the wet glue to resemble the miraculous star from the story.

Counting to Christmas

Capture the Christmas spirit of giving and sharing with a reading of *Counting to Christmas* by Nancy Tafuri (Scholastic Trade Books). As an extension to the story, place a small, artificial Christmas tree in the corner of your classroom. As you lead youngsters in making Christmas crafts, plan a session where youngsters can make two simple ornaments to hang on the tree. Just before winter break, invite parents to a Giving Tree Celebration. Have the children perform holiday songs, and then present each family with the two ornaments their child made for the tree. Suggest that each family keep one ornament for themselves and give the other to a neighbor, relative, or friend. End the celebration with cookies and hot chocolate to go with the warm feelings associated with your Giving Tree.

Christmas Time

Celebrate the merriment of preparing for Christmas through the eyes of a child in *Christmas Time* by Catherine Stock (Aladdin Paperbacks). After reading the story, revisit the illustration of the young girl making Christmas cookies. Then sharpen early scissors skills by inviting your little elves to make Christmas cookies from play dough. Add Christmas cookie cutters and rolling pins to your play dough area. To make a Christmas cookie, a child gently presses the cookie cutter of his choice onto rolled-out play dough to make an imprint. Then he removes the cookie cutter and uses scissors to cut out the shape. Encourage your little bakers to add decorations by pressing colorful beads or rickrack into the play dough cookies. Mmmm! Don't you just love the smell of Christmas cookies?

Where's Prancer?

Oh, dear! Santa has a reindeer missing in *Where's Prancer?* by Syd Hoff (HarperCollins Publishers, Inc.). Use this follow-up activity to sharpen skills with one-to-one correspondence. Make two copies of the reindeer and carrot patterns (page 204). Color the eight reindeer and eight carrots; then cut them out and attach felt to the back of each cutout. As you read the story a second time, pause on the page where Santa discovers that one reindeer is missing. Lay the book aside and use your flannelboard to find out how Santa came to that conclusion. Place seven reindeer on the flannelboard. Give eight children one carrot each, counting them as you distribute each one. Ask one of the eight children at a time to place her carrot next to a different reindeer. Discuss why there is one carrot left over. Then continue reading the story to find out where the missing reindeer has gone. After Prancer's return, repeat the flannelboard activity. Just add the eighth reindeer to the board and redistribute the carrots for a feeding time with a happy ending.

SNOW

4	✺ ✺ ✺ ✺
1	✺
6	✺ ✺ ✺ ✺ ✺ ✺
3	✺ ✺ ✺

Snow Prints

Watch youngsters' math skills snowball with this cool counting activity. For each child, fold a large sheet of blue construction paper in half twice; then unfold it to reveal four sections as shown. Program each section with a different numeral. Then ask each child to print the number of snowflakes corresponding to the numeral in each section. To make a snowflake, have the child dip the end of an empty thread spool into white paint and then stamp the spool onto his paper. After the paint dries, have each child count the total number of his snowflakes. Then help him record that numeral on the back of his paper. Brrr! It's a counting blizzard!

Catching Snowflakes

Capture the thrill of catching snowflakes with this hands-on math activity. Have each child fold and cut one or two coffee filters to create snowflakes. Collect the snowflakes in a white plastic trash bag, which serves as a snow cloud. Then seat one small group of youngsters at a time in a circle around a sturdy chair. Carefully stand on the chair, holding the snow cloud as you sing this song. At the appropriate time, empty the bag; then invite each child to catch as many falling snowflakes as possible. Ask her to count and report the number she catches. Then refill the snow cloud for another snowfall. At a later time, you might chart the number of each group's captured and missed snowflakes and then compare the results.

(sung to the tune of "Sing a Song of Sixpence")

See a cloud of snowflakes floating in the sky.
Let's all try to catch one. Let's give it a try!
When the cloud bursts open, the snowflakes will fall
   down.
How many snowflakes can you catch before they
   touch the ground?

ABC Snowmen

Enlist the help of these snowmen to review the alphabet. In advance, write the poem below on chart paper. Then program each of 26 die-cut snowmen with a different letter. Laminate the snowmen for durability; then place them in a pocket chart. Display the snowmen with the rhyme. Working with one small group at a time, recite the rhyme. Point to each letter as you name it. Then evenly distribute the snowmen to the group members. Challenge them to sequence the snowmen alphabetically in the pocket chart, using the rhyme as a reference when necessary.

A, B, C, D, E, F, G.
Meet our snowmen A to Z.
H, I, J, K, L, and M.
We can learn so much
   from them.
N, O, P, Q, R, S, T.
Use the letter on each
   tummy…
U, V, W, X, Y, Z.
To line them up alphabetically.

"Rappin' " Up for the Cold

Reinforce the names of body parts when little ones dress to "brrr-ave" this blizzard. Invite youngsters to imagine that a heavy snow is blowing around outdoors. Then, as you say this rap, have them put on each imaginary clothing item.

It's snowin'! It's blowin'!
   I want to go outside!
First I must dress in clothes
   that are right.
A hat on my head,
   so warm and tight.
A scarf round my neck
   so the wind won't bite.
A coat for my body and snow
   pants to match.
Mittens on my hands for
   the snow that I catch.
Boots on my feet to keep
   my toes warm too.
With all I'm wearing, it's a
   wonder I can move!

A Blanket of Snow

Use this idea to cover some important visual and reasoning skills. In advance, collect a white bed sheet and several items with recognizable shapes, such as a thick book, a large ball, and a handled basket. Show the items to the children; then have them close their eyes and imagine that a blizzard is blowing into your room. While their eyes are closed, cover one of the items with the sheet and remove the remaining items from sight. Then challenge youngsters to open their eyes and guess the identity of the "snow-covered" item. Then "blow" the snow away to reveal the mystery shape beneath it. Repeat the activity as student interest dictates, using items of different shapes.

149

SNOW

Snow Snips

Here's a cool and easy way for youngsters to make their own unique snowflakes at your art center. Stock the center with a large supply of coffee filters and several pairs of scissors. Show students how to fold a coffee filter three times to create a triangle. Then demonstrate how to snip away pieces from the sides of the triangle without cutting away an entire folded side. Unfold the coffee filter to reveal a unique snowflake. Students will create a flurry of snowflakes in no time at all!

To Eat or Not to Eat?

Children love to snack on snow, but is it clean enough to eat? To find out, set up a snow investigation center after a fresh snowfall. Prepare a snow-melting jar by pushing a large coffee filter into the top of a wide-mouthed jar to create a cup inside the jar. Secure the filter to the rim of the jar with a rubber band. Then collect a few cups of snow. Encourage the children to look closely at the snow and describe what they see. Place a scoop of snow in the coffee filter; then allow the snow to melt. Have children explore other centers while the snow melts, reminding them to periodically check the snow as it changes from a solid to a liquid. After the snow has melted completely, remove the coffee filter from the jar. Have students inspect the filter for color and debris. After this experiment, your students will conclude that snow only *looks* good enough to eat.

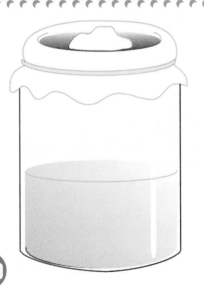

Sensational Sensory Snow

Invite youngsters to have mounds of fun with some faux snow. Remove the chairs from a classroom table so students can stand around it, and then protect the floor beneath the table with a sheet or newspaper. Squirt several mounds of shaving cream on the table and invite youngsters at the center to enjoy the piles of faux snow. Encourage children to draw in the snow or write letters, numerals, or their names. If desired, provide snowman cookie cutters. Every once in a while, create a fresh snowfall by squirting more shaving cream onto the table. When it's time to clean up for the next snow crew, just plow the mess away with the wipe of a wet cloth. It's guaranteed to be "snow" much fun—without the cold!

Shimmering "Snowdough"

Add some seasonal sparkle to your play-dough area with this glistening glitter snow. In advance, use your favorite recipe to make a batch of play dough, without adding color to it. Then sprinkle a layer of iridescent glitter on your play-dough table. Ask youngsters to roll the fresh batch of dough in the glitter. Encourage them to observe how the glitter adheres to the play dough, making it sparkle. Then invite youngsters to use their "snowdough" to form some sparkly snow creations.

Snow Matters

Use these cool cubes to help your little ones experience the meltdown of a solid into a liquid. To prepare, make a thin mixture of white tempera paint and water. Pour the thin paint into ice-cube trays; then add a craft stick to each cup. (Make at least one cube per student.) Place the trays in the freezer overnight. The next day, remove the paint cubes from the trays.

Place a few cubes in your art center; then return the remaining cubes to the freezer until students are ready to use them. Invite each youngster at the center to paint on a sheet of blue or black paper with a paint cube. As you circulate, ask youngsters to describe the changes in the cubes as they paint. What a beautiful meltdown!

SNOW

It's "Snow" Secret!

Invite your youngsters to have some frosty fun using their senses. To prepare, put fresh snow or crushed ice in a resealable plastic bag. Place the plastic bag in a brown paper bag and fold down the top. Have your youngsters form a circle; then hold up the bag for the class to see. Challenge the class to guess what is in the bag by using their senses. As you pass the bag around the circle, ask each child to grasp the top of the bag and describe how heavy it feels. Next invite the students to shake the bag and describe how it sounds. Then open the top of the bag and encourage your little ones to smell the contents without peeking. Bring a chilly end to this guessing game by inviting youngsters to reach inside and feel the cold snow. If desired, follow up with a treat for the eyes and taste buds—snow cones!

There's 'snowbody' like me!

"Snowbody" Like Me!

Youngsters will feel special when they discover that, just like snowflakes, no two children are alike. To prepare, fold and snip several coffee filters to make unique snowflake shapes. Glue each snowflake to a black construction-paper background, and display it for all to see. Explain to the class that scientists have never discovered two snowflakes that are alike. Then tell youngsters that they have something in common with snowflakes. Have each youngster turn to face another child. Invite the partners to look at each other and discuss physical characteristics, such as eye, hair, and skin color. Help each child conclude, "There's 'snowbody' just like me!"

152

Silly Snowmen

Give a lesson in listening as your youngsters size up these snowmen. In advance, cut from white polyester batting one small, one medium, and one large circle. Ask a student volunteer to place the circles randomly on your flannelboard as you call out each circle's size—small, medium, or large. Next ask the child to arrange the circles to form a snowman. If necessary, clarify concepts such as *bottom, top,* or *above.* Next have another volunteer follow your directions to arrange the circles differently on the flannelboard. As each subsequent volunteer creates an arrangement, invite youngsters to shout out the result—"Snowman!" or "No-man!"

I'm Melting!

Put stronger subtraction skills at your students' fingertips with this snowy song. Count down with repeated verses until the sun has melted every flake.

(sung to the tune of "Five Little Ducks")

[Five] snowflakes come out to play,   *(Hold up [five] fingers.)*
Down from the sky so far away.   *(Wiggle fingers downward.)*
Sunshine comes out strong and bright.   *(Wave other hand over five fingers.)*
One little flake melts out of sight.   *(Put one finger down.)*

All Dressed Up With "Snow-where" to Go

There's "snow" substitute for warm clothing on a snowy day. Sing the following song during circle time as your little ones act out bundling up in each article of clothing.

(sung to the tune of "The Farmer in the Dell")

It's cold outside today.
It's cold outside today.
Brrr! Brrr! It's cold outside!
Let's get dressed to play.

I put my snowsuit on.
I put my snowsuit on.
Brrr! Brrr! It's cold outside!
I put my snowsuit on.

Continue with other verses:

I put my snow boots on…
I put my mittens on…
I put my wool hat on…
I put my warm scarf on…

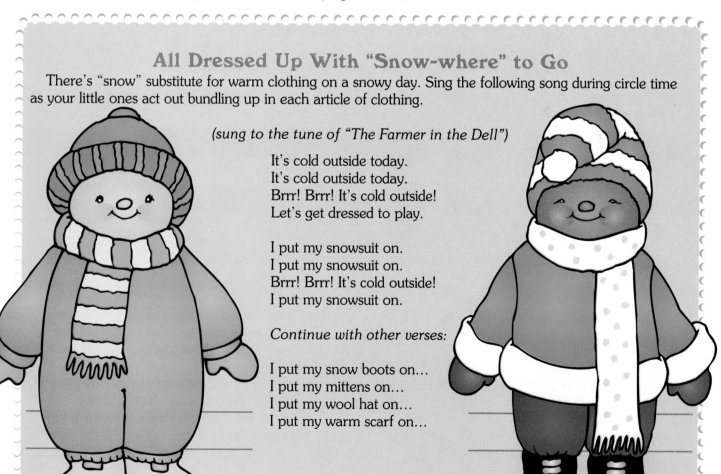

SNOW

Missing Mittens

Put your little kittens to work finding some lost mittens at your sensory table. Place a few pairs of mittens in the bottom of your sensory table; then fill the table with real snow or white Styrofoam® packing pieces. Add a few sand shovels to the table. Set up a clothesline nearby with a basket of spring-type clothespins. When small groups visit this center, encourage them to dig the mittens out with the shovels. Once the mittens are found, ask little ones to match the pairs; then have them hang the pairs on the line to dry.

A Sweet Snowstorm

Let it snow! Let it snow! Let it snow all over this miniature town! To prepare, pour a cup of powdered sugar into the bottom of a gift box. Line the box lid with a sheet of construction paper. Then place the boxes on a newspaper-covered table along with a sifter, a scoop, dollhouse people, small toy cars, small blocks, and toy trees. Invite each child in turn to create a scene inside the box lid with the provided items. Then ask him to scoop some sugar into the sifter. Have him hold the sifter over his town as he creates a sugary snowstorm by squeezing the sifter handle. When the storm is over, ask the child to carefully remove each item to find its snow shadow. Have him shake the snow off each item; then help him return the sugar to the other box. If desired, invite the child to repeat the activity, this time laying flat some of the items—such as the people or trees. After the next snowstorm passes, have him again remove the items to reveal different silhouettes.

154

Scoopin' Snowballs

Here's the latest scoop on how to squeeze in fine-motor skills—use ice-cream scoops! Collect a tub of snow and a supply of short, thin sticks. (If snow is not available, use white play dough.) Place the snow and sticks on a classroom table with some ice-cream scoops, Styrofoam® meat trays, raisins, and empty black film canisters. Invite each child at this center to use the ice-cream scoop to make three snowballs. Have her stack her snowballs on a tray to make a snowman. Then encourage her to add a film-canister hat, a raisin face, and raisin buttons to her snowman. Invite the child to complete her snowman with a pair of stick arms. Now that's a chilly way to have fun!

Gearing Up for Snow

Here's a wintry way to warm up fine-motor and self-help skills at the same time. Gather winter jackets, sweaters, snow pants, boots, and any other type of winter wear with fasteners such as zippers, buckles, snaps, buttons, or laces. Put the gear in your dramatic-play area along with a timer. Set the timer for a designated amount of time; then invite a small group of youngsters to suit up in the winter gear. Encourage each child to fasten one article of clothing before putting on the next. When there's "snow" time left on the clock, invite the children to take an imaginary frolic in the snow. Whee!

Winter Wonderland Mural

Creating this snowy mural is sure to add up to a blizzard of fun for youngsters! Tape a length of blue bulletin-board paper to a long classroom table. Or place the paper on a newspaper-covered area of your classroom floor. Invite youngsters to dip small paint rollers into white tempera paint; then have them roll a white blanket of snow along the bottom of the paper. Show them how to make snowmen by pressing white shoe-polish circles on the paper. Once the paint is dry, encourage little ones to use markers to add features to their snowmen. Have them peel and stick white sticky dots onto the paper to represent a snowfall; then invite students to add their own chalk drawings of sledders, skiers, and other snowy-fun scenes.

SNOW

Snowball Knockdown

Knock-knock. Who's there? Snow. Snow who? "Snow-one" can resist this fun activity! In advance, collect about a dozen clean, empty soda bottles (or milk cartons). Then take youngsters outdoors on a snowy day. Line up the soda bottles, with plenty of space between them. Have your students line up side by side some distance away from the line of bottles. Invite each child to make a snowball and then throw it at a bottle, attempting to knock it down. Periodically replace the knocked-down bottles and keep the snowballs coming for more practice with throwing and hand-eye coordination.

Snow Crew

Shovel up some fun by turning your class into a road crew in charge of snow removal. Gather a few sand shovels, toy dump trucks and/or toy bulldozers, a few small containers (such as cake tins or shoeboxes), a broom, and a large garbage bag of white Styrofoam® peanuts (the peanuts can be purchased from a mailing-supplies store).

On a windless day, bring a group of students outdoors to a concrete or blacktop area; then divide the group into pairs. Give one child in each pair a container filled with Styrofoam® peanuts. Then instruct him to make it snow by lifting his container in the air and tossing the peanuts over his partner's head. Then pass out a shovel or toy truck to each pair. Partners can either take turns shoveling the snow or using the truck to dump snow into the container. Once the container is full, have the partners switch roles and make it snow again. When it's time to clean up, have your road crew shovel, plow, and sweep the snow back into the garbage bag as you hold it. Then truck on inside to get out of the cold!

MOVEMENT

Snowball Hoopla

How about playing a little hoop in the snow? Snowball hoop, that is! Gather plastic hoops for half your group. Take the children outdoors on a snowy day and divide the group into pairs. Ask the partners to stand about five feet apart; then give one child in each pair a hoop. Ask him to hold it to his side, resembling a basketball goal. Have his partner form a snowball and try to toss it through the hoop. For variety, have the hoop holder hold the hoop vertically (lion-tamer-style) as his partner attempts to toss a snowball through it. After a few throws, have the partners trade places.

If you'd like both partners to toss snowballs at the same time, have them place their hoop on the ground some distance away. Have them try to toss their snowballs into the hoop. Once they're successful, challenge them to move the hoop a bit farther away.

Snow Foolin'

If throwing real snowballs is a safety concern, try this alternative. You will need one sheet of white tissue paper for each student and a few cardboard boxes. Bring your class and materials outdoors. Pass out the tissue paper and ask each youngster to crumple his sheet to resemble a snowball. Encourage youngsters to aim their snowballs at objects like trees, bushes, or walls, but caution them not to throw these snowball substitutes—or real snowballs—at people. For a flurry of fun, make boxes available for students to toss their snowballs into from a distance. Let the snowballs fly!

Beach-Ball Snowballs

Watch your youngsters' enthusiasm snowball with this cool activity! Gather enough beach balls for half your class. Go outdoors to an open field and divide the class into partners. As you pass out a beach ball to each pair, ask them to imagine that it is a giant snowball. Invite each set of partners to cooperatively roll their snowball forward, backward, and sideways. Encourage each pair to take turns lying on the snowball by balancing themselves on their stomachs. Can they toss or roll the snowball back and forth to each other? Next, group three pairs of students together to see whether they can stack their three snowballs on top of each other to make a snowman. It's hard to believe "snow" much fun can be rolled into one activity!

SNOW

Sweet Snowflake

Ingredients:
2 Pizzelle Italian-style cookies per child
whipped topping
powdered sugar

Utensils and Supplies:
napkins
spoon
small sieve

Teacher Preparation:
   Arrange the ingredients and utensils near the step-by-step direction cards.

What to Do When the Snack Is Through

Use some leftover Pizzelle cookies to make shimmering snowflake prints. Provide blue construction paper, silver glitter, and a shallow container of white tempera paint. Encourage each youngster to dip a cookie into the paint and then press it onto his paper. Then have him shake silver glitter onto the wet paint.

As a variation, mix some dish detergent into the white paint; then make some Pizzelle prints on your classroom windows to give your classroom a frosty glow!

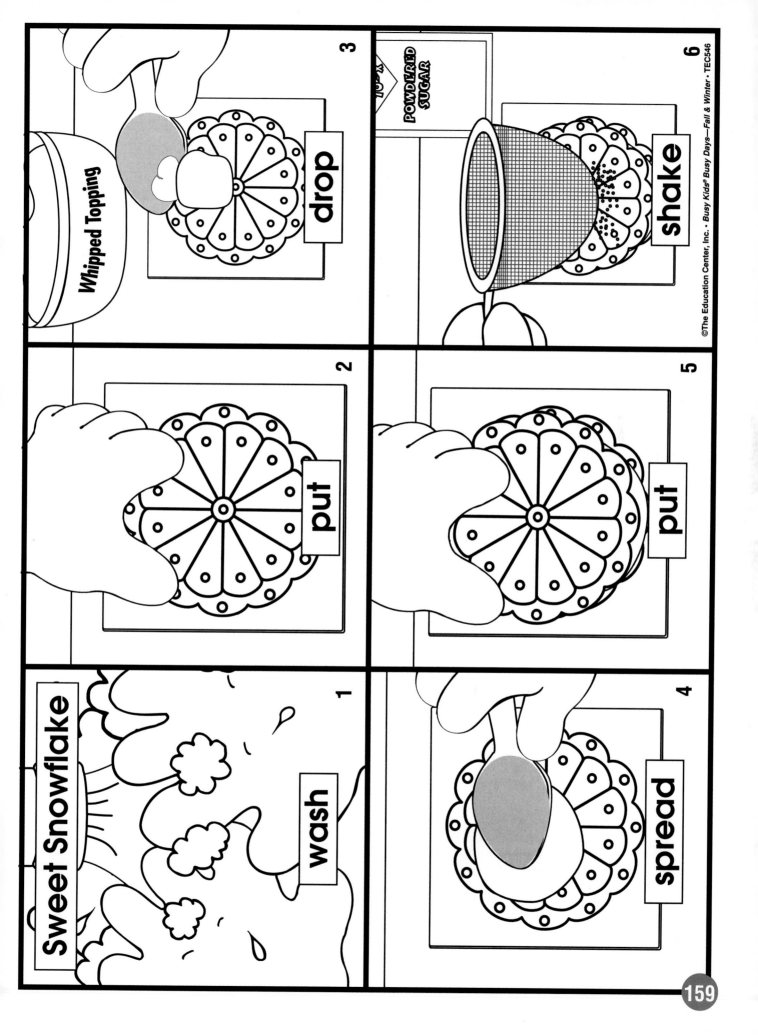

Sweet Snowflake

wash **1**

put **2**

Whipped Topping

drop **3**

spread **4**

put **5**

POWDERED SUGAR

shake **6**

©The Education Center, Inc. • *Busy Kids® Busy Days—Fall & Winter* • TEC546

SNOW

Snowflakes Landing

One little snowflake falling from the sky,
Landing in a treetop, oh-so-high.

Sway one finger.
Touch finger to extended arm.

Two little snowflakes drifting to the ground,
Landing on the street without a sound.

Sway two fingers.
Move fingers down to floor.

Three little snowflakes hurry by so fast,
Landing on people as they rush past.

Sway three fingers.
Move fingers to shoulder.

Four little snowflakes whirling all around,
Landing in a heap on the chilly ground.

Sway four fingers.
Move fingers down to floor.

Five little snowflakes falling as I sleep,
Adding to the snow that's white and deep.

Sway five fingers.
Move fingers down to floor; then hold palm flat above the floor to indicate deep.

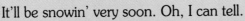
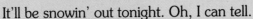
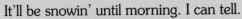

It'll Be Snowin' Very Soon

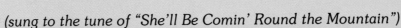

(sung to the tune of "She'll Be Comin' Round the Mountain")

It'll be snowin' very soon. Oh, I can tell.
It'll be snowin' very soon. Oh, I can tell.
It'll be snowin' very soon. There's a ring around the moon.
It'll be snowin' very soon. Oh, I can tell.

It'll be snowin' out tonight. Oh, I can tell.
It'll be snowin' out tonight. Oh, I can tell.
It'll be snowin' out tonight. The forecast says I'm right.
It'll be snowin' out tonight. Oh, I can tell.

It'll be snowin' until morning. I can tell.
It'll be snowin' until morning. I can tell.
It'll be snowin' until morning. No school, cause winter's storming!
It'll be snowin' until morning. I can tell.

Snowy Day

*(sung to the tune of
"Jingle Bells")*

Sledding fast, sledding fast,
Down the hilly way.
Oh, what fun it is to play
On a bright and snowy day!

Snow angels, snow angels,
Everywhere I lay.
Oh, what fun it is to play
On a bright and snowy day!

Snowman Tale

I am a snowman   Point to self.
Standing on the lawn.   Stand with hands on hips.
The sun comes out,   Shield eyes as you look up.
And now I am gone.   Pretend to melt.

White and Fluffy Stuff

(sung to the tune of "Are You Sleeping?")

It is snowing! It is snowing!
Come on, all! Come on, all!
Do you think there is enough
Of this white and fluffy stuff
For snowballs, for snowballs?

It is snowing! It is snowing!
Oh, how grand! Oh, how grand!
Do you think there is enough
Of this white and fluffy stuff
For a snowman, for a snowman?

It is snowing! It is snowing!
Oh, what fun! Oh, what fun!
Yes, there surely is enough
Of this white and fluffy stuff!
The fun's begun! The fun's begun!

SNOW

Millions of Snowflakes

Count on Mary McKenna Siddals' *Millions of Snowflakes* (Clarion Books) to warm up even the coldest day. This playful counting poem progresses from one snowflake to millions of gently falling snowflakes. For a frosty followup, set up a snowflake center with white tempera paint, iridescent glitter, a shallow box, and wagon wheel pasta (or thread spools). Fold large sheets of blue or lavender construction paper in half. On one half of each folded sheet of paper, write the numerals 1 to 5 in a column. On the other half, write "Millions of Snowflakes."

At this center, a child dips the pasta (or spool) into the paint and then stamps the corresponding number of snowflakes beside each numeral. On the side labeled "Millions of Snowflakes," the child stamps snowflakes to her heart's content. Then she places her paper inside the box and sprinkles the wet snowflakes with iridescent glitter. You'll see millions of sparkling snowflakes falling everywhere!

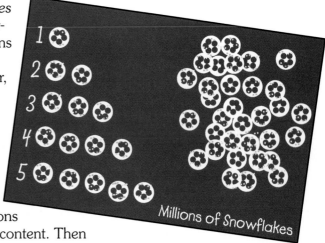

Millions of Snowflakes

The Snowy Day

Delight in the wonders of the deep, deep snow with a reading of Ezra Jack Keats' *The Snowy Day* (Viking Press). This Caldecott Medal winner is an absolute "must read" after a fresh snowfall. After sharing this snowy tale, invite your little ones to try this snowy science experiment. Bring in buckets of snow to fill your water table (or fill the table with crushed ice). Make a snowball and place it in a resealable plastic bag. Then put the bag inside a coat pocket. Hang the coat where youngsters can reach it, so that they can pull the snowball from the pocket to see whether it melts as Peter's did in the story. While the children are waiting for the snowball to disappear, invite them to enjoy the frosty fun in the water table.

Snowballs

What can you do with a snowball? Make snowfolks, of course! Lois Ehlert's *Snowballs* (Harcourt Brace & Company) is chock-full of snow people and snow animals made with a little help from some "good stuff in a sack." If there is snow where you live, gather your own "good stuff" and take it outdoors on a snowy day to decorate snow figures that your youngsters make in the snow. Then, if you're hungry from all that snowperson building, follow the recipe at the end of the book for making popcorn balls. Or make these yummy snowfolk faces. Gather a class supply of popcorn (or rice) cakes, white cream cheese (or frosting), and small bowls of edible "good stuff," such as raisins, M&Ms® candies, pretzels, or popped popcorn. Invite each child to spread cream cheese on his popcorn cake and then use the other items to make an original snow person or snow animal face.

Elmer in the Snow

David McKee's *Elmer in the Snow* (Lothrop, Lee & Shepard Books) is sure to be a big hit as your youngsters watch Elmer introduce his elephant friends to their first snow experience. If your youngsters are unfamiliar with Elmer, be sure to share David McKee's other Elmer adventures with the class. Then follow up with this elephant extension. Set up your art table with colored and white construction paper, glue, scissors, markers, salt, and paintbrushes. Make a mixture of half salt and half water. Use the pattern on page 205 to cut several Elmer patterns from tagboard.

At this center, a child traces and then cuts two Elmer patterns from white construction paper. He paints one elephant with the salt mixture to make a frozen Elmer. While his painting is drying, he uses a light-colored marker to make vertical and horizontal lines on his other elephant cutout. Then he uses markers to color in the squares to resemble the patchwork Elmer. Finally, he folds a sheet of colored paper in half and glues one Elmer to each half. "Weather" in the snow or sun, Elmer is always lots of fun!

Rainsong/Snowsong

Rainsong/Snowsong by Philemon Sturges (North-South Books Inc.) is a joyful celebration of a summer's rain and a winter's snow in delightful rhyming text. This book, with its irresistible illustrations, provides the perfect opportunity to discuss rainwear and snow gear. After reading the story, revisit the illustrations, calling youngsters' attention to the clothing. Then gather these clothes from the rainsong: a rain slicker, a pair of boots, and a rain hat (or umbrella). Collect these clothes from the snowsong: a scarf, a pair of mittens, and a snow hat. Put the clothing in your dramatic-play area and encourage youngsters to sort the clothing into a rainsong stack and a snowsong stack. Then invite them to try on the clothes and pretend to frolic in the rain and snow.

163

Valentine's Day

Rhymin' Time for Valentines

Leave it to these valentine poems to sweeten your youngsters' rhyming skills. Copy the poems onto paper. Make enough copies so that each child will have one poem. Then play a simple rhyming game with your class. Simply say a word; then ask students to name words that rhyme with the word. Afterward share these poems. Ask youngsters to supply the missing word in each one. Then give each child a copy of one of the poems. Help him write the missing word in the blank. Invite him to glue his poem onto a large construction paper heart and then to decorate it with valentine stickers. Encourage him to deliver his poem to his favorite valentine.

Valentine, valentine,
Please be true.
Valentine, valentine,
I love _____. *(you)*

Valentine, valentine,
Please be mine.
Valentine, valentine,
You're so _____. *(fine)*

Valentine, valentine,
You're so sweet.
Valentine, valentine,
You knock me off my _____. *(feet)*

> Valentine, valentine,
> Please be true.
> Valentine, valentine,
> I love __you__.

Opposites Attract

Attract attention to opposites with these valentine puzzles. Cut out a supply of construction paper hearts equal to half the number of children in your class. Program each side of the cutout with a word from an opposite pair. (If desired, add picture clues for younger children.) Then puzzle-cut each heart cutout to create two halves.

Show the hearts to the group, discussing each pair of opposites. Then mix up the heart halves and give one to each child. Help him read the word on his puzzle piece before having him search for the child with its opposite. When two children complete their heart puzzle, have them sit together in your group area. Then review the opposite pairs once more.

164

	Rodney	Kenny	Who has more?
pink 🩷	2	3	Kenny
white 🤍	1	0	Rodney
green 💚	4	2	Rodney
yellow 💛	0	2	Kenny
orange 🧡	3	3	Same

My "Sweet-chart"

Kindergartners will think this categorizing and counting activity is a colorful, tasty treat! In advance, make a chart similar to the one shown; then make one copy for every two children in your class. Place the charts and a supply of candy hearts in a center. To use the center, each child in a student pair writes his name on the chart. The partners read the color words in the first column and then color each heart the corresponding color. Then each child takes ten candy hearts. He sorts his candy by color. Then he counts the number of each heart color and writes that numeral in the appropriate box on the chart. Afterward, the partners compare their quantities for each color. The child with the larger amount writes his name in the corresponding box. Invite each pair to end this activity in a sweet way—by eating the candy hearts. Yum!

Hearty Handshake

Pass along some number fun with these hearty handshakes. Cut out a class supply of small red construction paper hearts; then label each heart with a different numeral from 1 up to the number of children in your class. Explain that you will show each child how to give a hearty handshake. Before shaking his hand, slip a heart cutout into your palm. Then heartily shake the child's hand, pressing the heart into his palm. After every child receives a handshake and a heart, have youngsters identify the numerals on their hearts. Then invite them to sequence themselves into a valentine number line.

You're All Heart

Introduce some new body parts vocabulary with this activity that's all heart...and chest...and knees...and elbows! To prepare, cut out a red construction paper heart for each child. Distribute the cutouts; then ask your little valentines to use them to perform this heartfelt song.

(sung to the tune of "If You're Happy and You Know It")

Put your heart on your chest, on your chest.
Put your heart on your chest, on your chest.
Put your heart on your chest 'cause that's where it fits the best.
Put your heart on your chest, on your chest.

Put your heart on your knee, on your knee.
Put your heart on your knee, on your knee.
Put your heart on your knee—what a silly place to be.
Put your heart on your knee, on your knee.

Continue with other verses, replacing the body part and the last part of the third line with one of the following:

elbow...like a funny little fellow.
calf...then giggle, giggle, laugh.
thigh...then give a little sigh.

Valentine's Day

Wedding Bells

Valentine's Day is near and love is in the air! To celebrate, fill your dramatic-play center with all sorts of wedding clothes. Collect old suit jackets, formal dresses, scarves, high heels, plastic flower bouquets, and other wedding accessories. If desired, create a bridal veil from inexpensive netting and a child's headband. Then place the wedding attire in your center, along with a tape of the classic "Here Comes the Bride." Boys and girls alike will enjoy getting groomed during this month of love.

Susan Hodnett

Sea of Love

Zip up some learning about magnets with this discovery-center idea. To prepare, cut several heart shapes from sheets of craft foam or from brightly colored, plastic party cups. Attach a paper clip diagonally across each heart (to resemble an arrow). Place the clipped hearts into a quart-size zippered plastic bag; then partially fill the bag with red-tinted water. Carefully squeeze out any excess air; then seal the bag and add a strip of masking tape to prevent leaks. Make one or more of these bags as desired. Place the bag (or bags), along with a few magnets, in your discovery center. Invite youngsters to use the magnets to move the hearts through the water. Little ones will be attracted to this center!

Valentines to Go

Invite youngsters to your art center to decorate these "heart-y" valentine-collection boxes. In advance, gather a class supply of cardboard laundry-detergent boxes with flip tops. Cover each box with white butcher paper. Put the covered boxes in your art center, along with a large supply of colored tissue-paper hearts, heart-shaped confetti, some paintbrushes, and a mixture of two parts glue and one part water.

At this center, invite each child to paint the glue mixture onto the sides and top of her box, then cover her box with tissue hearts and confetti. Allow time for the boxes to dry before attaching a ribbon handle to each one. Invite youngsters to use their boxes to collect valentine sweets and treats from their classmates during your Valentine's Day festivities.

Candy Counting

Counting candy in the math center is sure to sweeten youngsters' skills with one-to-one correspondence. To prepare, gather several egg cartons. Cut one-cup to ten-cup segments from the cartons. Then place the egg-carton segments and a container of small candy hearts in the math center. Have each youngster select an egg-carton segment; then ask her to count the number of cups in the segment. Invite her to count out a corresponding number of candy hearts. Have her place one heart into each cup to check the accuracy of her counting. Then invite her to again count each sweet treat—as she pops them into her mouth to eat!

Patterns of the Heart

Here's a "scent-sible" and seasonal way to practice patterning. To begin, make a batch of red, cherry-scented play dough. Then use large and small heart-shaped cookie cutters to trace repeating patterns onto a quantity of sentence strips. (Leave room on each strip so that youngsters can continue the pattern.) Laminate the pattern strips for durability. Then place the pattern strips, the cookie cutters, and the play dough in a center.

At this center, a child cuts large and small hearts from the play dough, then lays these hearts on a strip to extend the pattern.

Cherry Play Dough
2 1/2 cups flour
1 cup salt
1 tablespoon cream of tartar
2 packages unsweetened cherry Kool-Aid®
3 tablespoons cooking oil
2 cups boiling water

Mix the dry ingredients. Add the oil and boiling water. Stir quickly, mixing well. When cool, mix with your hands. Store in an airtight container.

Valentine's Day

Be My Valentine!

Mystery Valentine

Have your youngsters send "love-ly" sentiments one another's way with this valentine game. Set a chair at a distance from the children. Invite one child to sit in the chair with his back to the class. Silently signal another child to stand directly behind—but out of the sight of—the child in the chair. Have her disguise her voice and say, "Be my valentine." Then have her sit back down. Watch for giggles and grins as the child in the chair tries to identify his secret admirer. After the secret has been revealed, have the two players exchange places; then select another child to send a hearty greeting.

A Heartfelt Song

This color-review song will have your little songbirds singing with all their hearts. Purchase a bag of large candy conversation hearts. Identify the color of each heart as you give one to each child. Then sing the following song repeated times, substituting the various colors of the candy hearts.

(sung to the tune of "Where Is Thumbkin?")

Teacher:	Where is [pink] heart? Where is [pink] heart?	
Students:	Here I am! Here I am!	*Children with pink hearts stand and sing.*
All:	Happy Val-en-tine's Day! Happy Val-en-tine's Day!	
Teacher:	Eat your heart. Now sit down.	*Children eat hearts.* *Children sit down.*

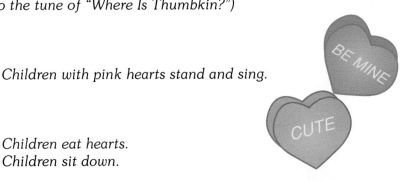

Special Delivery

Make distributing valentines carefree instead of chaotic with this tip. In advance tape a school photo (or other close-up photo) of each child to a sheet of copy paper. Duplicate a copy of the resulting class gallery for each child. To each copy, attach a note to parents requesting that they assist their children in cutting out the pictures and pasting them to the fronts of their valentine envelopes.

During your valentine celebration, invite a few children at a time to distribute their valentines, using the photos on their envelopes to guide them as they make their special deliveries.

Valentine History

Share some valentine history with your little sweethearts. Long ago, ladies' names were written on pretty slips of paper and placed in a glass jar. Gentlemen would come forward and draw a name from the jar. The lady whose name was drawn became his valentine. Another valentine custom was that a gentleman would wear his valentine's name on his sleeve for several days. (The saying "wearing his heart on his sleeve" probably came from this tradition.)

Try this modified version of these bygone customs. Write your children's names on construction-paper hearts and place them in a large jar. Invite one child at a time to select a name from the jar; then use masking tape to attach the name to his sleeve. Next give him a candy heart to present to his chosen valentine. Encourage your young gentlemen and ladies to be kind and thoughtful to their sweetheart friends for the remainder of the day.

Broken Hearts

Mend broken hearts while strengthening number sense with this matching activity. Cut enough large heart shapes from construction paper for half your class. Program one side of each heart with a numeral and the other side with a corresponding set of hearts. Then cut each paper heart up the middle between the numeral and its corresponding set of hearts. Put the broken hearts in a box and mix them up.

Have the class form a circle; then distribute one half of a heart to each child. Ask the class to hold up their broken hearts for all to see. Challenge each youngster to find the missing half of his heart. Once a child has found a classmate with his heart's missing half, invite the pair to stand side by side and mend the broken heart. In the following days, reinforce other basic skills in a heartbeat by programming a new set of hearts with rhyming pictures or upper- and lowercase letters.

169

Valentine's Day

Laced With Love

Do your youngsters love to lace? Then prepare this lacing center to provide some Valentine's Day fine-motor fun. To prepare, purchase large plastic needles and sheets of plastic canvas (available at craft stores). Cut an assortment of heart shapes from each sheet of canvas; then snip off any jagged edges. Place red, white, and pink yarn in a center with the canvas hearts and the needles. (If desired, substitute pipe cleaners for the yarn and needles.) Invite each student at this center to cut a length of yarn; then help her thread one end of the yarn through the eye of a needle. Have her tie the other end of the yarn to the canvas heart. Encourage her to lace the yarn around the perimeter of the heart shape or to create a yarn design of her own. After she receives some "heart-y" compliments from you and from the other children at this center, ask her to remove the yarn for the next child who wishes to do some lovely lacing.

"Syrup-n-dipity"

Give fingers a sweet workout with this finger-lickin'-good activity. To prepare, purchase a squeeze bottle of strawberry syrup and a class supply of thick paper plates. Encourage each child to squeeze a thin layer of strawberry syrup onto a plate. Have him tilt the plate back and forth to cover the bottom of the plate with a smooth layer of syrup. Then encourage him to use his index finger to draw hearts in the syrup. If desired, provide candy conversation hearts with simple sentiments, such as "Be Mine" or "I Love You." Invite each child to copy the words in his syrup. Remind children to tilt their plates to spread the syrup into a smooth layer each time they wish to make new drawings or words. When they're finished with this activity, invite them to lick their fingers clean. Yummy!

Heart Art

Take heart! Here are a few simple ways to teach your little ones how to draw their own hearts. To begin, have each child fold a sheet of paper in half. Then have her place a thumb at an angle on the fold. Help her trace her thumb—starting and ending at the fold—to create the outline of half a heart. Or have her substitute the end of a large craft stick for her thumb. Or show her how to draw an angled candy cane on the paper fold. Invite the child to make several tracings. Then have her cut out her outlines, unfold the cut-outs, and decorate her hearts as she desires. Invite her to glue her hearts onto a construction-paper background to create a design or picture. Now that's art with heart!

Valentine Crayons

Your little ones will melt a lot of hearts when they create these valentines made from recycled crayons. To begin, gather several small, single-serving pie tins. Mold each tin into the shape of a heart. (Be careful not to crack the tin.) Then invite students to gather broken red, pink, and purple crayons. Have them peel the paper off the crayons. Then ask youngsters to break the crayons into small pieces. Have them sort the crayons by color, filling each tin to the rim. Heat the crayon-filled tins in a 250° oven until the crayons melt into a soft, but not watery, substance (about 5–10 minutes). When the crayon hearts cool, remove them from the tins. Then provide youngsters with heart cutouts from different materials, such as sandpaper, plastic canvas, and textured wallpaper samples. Invite each child to use the special valentine crayons and cutouts to make heart rubbings on a sheet of paper. Lovely!

Valentine Finger Folly

Your youngsters will fall in love with these valentine finger puppets! For each child, copy onto red or pink construction paper one large heart, one medium heart, and two small hearts from the patterns on page 206. Cut two six-inch strips of pink or red construction paper for each child.

Invite each child in a small group to make a finger puppet. To make one, cut out all the hearts. Punch holes as indicated on the large heart; then cut slits as indicated to make larger openings. Draw heart-shaped facial features on the medium cutout. Then glue the face onto the point of the large heart. Next, accordion-fold each paper strip. To make arms for the puppet, glue a small heart to one end of each paper strip; then glue the other end of each strip to the large heart. To give the puppet legs, poke your index and middle fingers through the holes in the large heart. Encourage each child, in turn, to lead the class as she makes her puppet walk, kick, march, or slide to this rhyme.

Move it to the right.
Move it to the left.
Move it in the way
Your heart loves best.

susan
Hodnett

171

Valentine's Day

"Valentubes"

Add a little heart to your art with these "valentube" streamers. Provide an empty toilet-paper tube for each child. Encourage children to paint their tubes with pink, red, white, or purple paint. After the paint is dry, have each child glue small paper hearts to his tube. Next give each student three 2-foot strips of pink, red, white, or purple crepe paper. Direct each child to glue one end of each of his streamers to the inside of his tube. Then invite your youngsters to move with their valentine "valentubes" to this heartwarming action rhyme:

[Hop, hop, hop] with your valentine. *Hop on one foot.*
[Hop] with your valentine now. *Make streamer hop.*

Refrain:
Valentine up, *Hold streamer up in the air.*
Valentine down, *Hold streamer down by side.*
Valentine, valentine, all around! *Circle streamer overhead.*

Repeat the rhyme as many times as desired, substituting other action words—such as *wiggle, walk, jump, creep, march, dance, kick,* or *twirl*—for the underlined word. Just beware! This movement activity is bound to make hearts skip a beat!

Ya Gotta Have Heart!

Try this Valentine's Day version of Musical Chairs. Give each child a large red heart cut from a sheet of 9" x 12" construction paper. Ask children to form a circle and place their paper hearts at their feet. Then use a drum to imitate the sound of a heartbeat. As you beat the drum, demonstrate how to move in a clockwise direction around the circle of hearts. Tell youngsters that when the heartbeat stops, each child should find a heart and stand on it. After the first round of play, remove one or more of the paper hearts before resuming the drumbeat. Invite children who are without hearts to sit inside the circle and give their classmates a hearty round of applause!

Heartthrob

How about some heart-pumping exercise for your little heartthrobs? Use chalk to draw a large heart on an outdoor concrete or blacktop area. (Or use red masking or electrical tape on a floor or carpet indoors.) Have children follow your lead as you move in various ways around the heart outline. Hop, jump, stomp, crawl, tiptoe, or walk backwards. After leading several movements, give each child a turn to be the leader. Your little ones are sure to have a heartfelt good time!

Celebrating Couples

Your youngsters will fall in love with this singing and dancing activity! First ask children to brainstorm a list of famous couples from their favorite stories, such as Simba and Nala, Mickey and Minnie, and Cinderella and the prince. Write each character's name on a piece of heart-shaped paper; then put all the names in a basket. Ask each child to pick a name from the basket. Read aloud each child's pick to help him remember his identity for the activity to follow. Then invite everyone to form a circle and perform a Valentine's Day version of the Hokey-Pokey.

Before you begin each verse, call one couple to the center of the circle. Ask the couple to choose a movement appropriate for their characters. Continue until each couple has had the opportunity to lead this "love-ly" song!

(sung to the tune of "The Hokey-Pokey")

[Put your right paw in; put your right paw out.]
[Put your right paw in and shake it all about.]
We're celebrating couples as we turn ourselves around;
That's what love's all about!

A Hearty Workout

Little hearts will beat wildly over this exercise activity. Have your youngsters pair up; then ask a volunteer to select a motion—such as twirling, hopping, or dancing—to accompany the following song:

(sung to the tune of "Do You Know the Muffin Man?")

Oh, Valentine, come [dance] with me,
[Dance] with me, [dance] with me.
Oh, Valentine, come [dance] with me.
We'll [dance] and then we'll stop!

After a few rounds, have children put their hands over their hearts. As they feel the pounding in their chests, explain that exercise provides a workout for the heart, making it healthy and strong.

173

Valentine's Day

Love Bug

Ingredients:
1 red Jell-O® Jigglers® heart shape per child
2 candy conversation hearts per child
1 slice of kiwi per child
red string licorice

Utensils and Supplies:
1 small paper plate per child
knife
spatula
heart-shaped cookie cutter

Teacher Preparation:
Follow the package directions to make a batch of Jell-O® Jigglers®. Use a small heart-shaped cookie cutter to cut one heart from the gelatin for each child. Peel the necessary number of kiwi and cut them into slices; then cut the slices in half. Cut the string licorice into three-inch strands. Arrange the ingredients and utensils near the step-by-step direction cards.

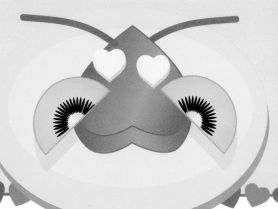

What to Do When the Snack Is Through

Youngsters are bound to put their hearts into this prereading activity. Place your leftover candy conversation hearts on a tray. Be sure the words on each heart are showing. Then invite youngsters to match the candy hearts that bear the same sentiment. As a challenge for older students, read the sentiment on an unidentified heart. Then see if your youngsters can locate the heart that you quoted.

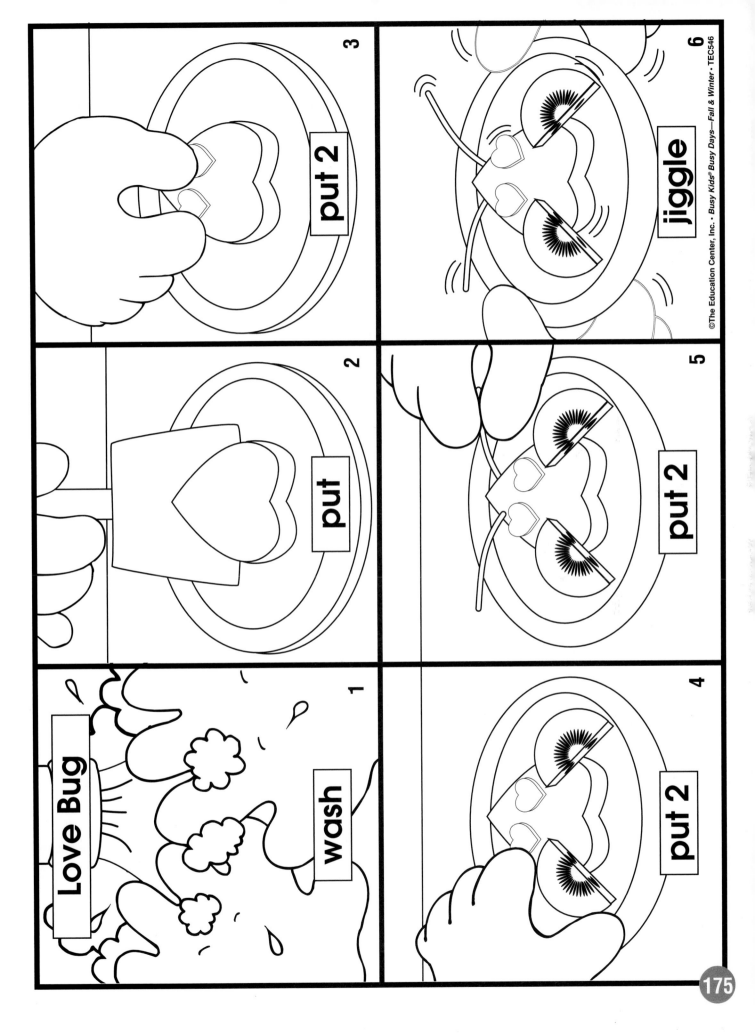

3

put 2

6

jiggle

©The Education Center, Inc. • Busy Kids® Busy Days—Fall & Winter • TEC546

2

put

5

put 2

Love Bug

1

wash

4

put 2

Valentine's Day

Hearts for You

Get ready to strengthen color recognition skills with this festive flannelboard song. In advance, cut one red, one pink, and one white heart from felt. Spread glue on the white heart, and then sprinkle it with gold glitter. After the glue dries, have your class sing the song. Invite a different volunteer to place the appropriate heart for each verse on your flannelboard. If desired, provide different felt heart colors; then create a verse for each additional color.

(sung to the tune of "The Farmer in the Dell")

A big heart made in red.
A big heart made in red.
Valentine, for you I have
A big heart made in red.

A big heart made in pink.
A big heart made in pink.
Valentine, for you I have
A big heart made in pink.

A big heart made in gold.
A big heart made in gold.
Valentine, for you I have
A big heart made in gold.

They're filled with love for you.
They're filled with love for you.
Valentine, these hearts I have
Are filled with love for you.

Valentines in All Sizes

Encourage your little sweethearts to sing this valentine verse three times. Have them whisper it the first time. Then change the word *teeny-tiny* to *medium,* and encourage students to sing at a normal volume for the second round. In the last round, substitute the words *great big huge*. Then have youngsters shout out this valentine news!

(sung to the tune of "On Top of Old Smokey")

I made a valentine,
Of [teeny-tiny] size
I made a valentine,
It's a sweet surprise!

A Fine Valentine Shine

(sung to the tune of "Rise and Shine")

Rise and shine,
And be my little valentine.
Rise and shine,
And be my little valentine.
Rise and shine and—

Be my valentine.
You are my true love!

Wave fingers overhead.
Put hands over heart.
Wave fingers overhead.
Put hands over heart.
*Wave fingers overhead. Clap
   once; then pause.*
Put hands over heart.
Point to friend; then point to self.

Send a Little Love

Deliver some fun to your youngsters with this valentine activity. To prepare, decorate three heart cutouts with stickers to create valentines. Then seat your little ones in a circle. Give a valentine to each of three children. As your class sings this song, instruct each child with a valentine to deliver it to a friend in the circle. Then repeat the song, having the three recipients deliver the valentines to three different friends. Continue in this manner until each child has made and received a very special valentine delivery.

*(sung to the tune of
"Jack and Jill")*

Valentine,
Oh, Valentine,
I have a gift—it's true!
You're my friend,
And so I send
This love-filled card to you!

177

Valentine's Day

Froggy's First Kiss

When Froggy receives an unexpected display of affection, his heart plays leapfrog in Jonathan London's *Froggy's First Kiss* (Viking Children's Books). After sharing this sweet story, invite each youngster to make a Froggy or a Frogilina from heart shapes. To prepare, cut two heart-shaped patterns from tagboard, making one tall and thin and the other short and wide. Cut a pair of large ovals from white construction paper for each child. Also cut lengths of orange and yellow curling ribbon and a supply of construction paper hair bows.

To make a frog, trace the heart shapes onto a 12" x 18" sheet of green construction paper; then cut them out. Glue the short, wide heart to the bottom half of the tall, thin heart to make the frog's face. Glue the white oval eyes to the top of the face. Use a black crayon to draw pupils and a big grin. To turn the frog into Frogilina, tape several pieces of curling ribbon to the back side of the frog's head; then curl them with scissors to create curls. Glue a decorated construction paper bow to the top of the frog's head. To finish off each Froggy, invite the child to put on some red lipstick before planting a big juicy kiss on Froggy's face!

Arthur's Valentine

Your little cupids will be tickled pink to discover Arthur's secret admirer in *Arthur's Valentine* by Marc Brown (Little, Brown and Company). After reading the story, invite youngsters to play this guessing game involving their own secret admirers. To prepare, draw a heart on a sheet of paper; then write this message on the heart: "Your secret admirer is wearing _____." Photocopy a class supply of the heart onto red construction paper. Have each child cut out a heart; then help him fill in the blank with a brief description of what he is wearing. Encourage him to decorate the heart with valentine stickers; then help him tape a candy kiss to the heart. Once all the hearts are complete, place them in a valentine gift bag. Invite one child at a time to select a heart from the bag; then say the following poem together. Read the message on the heart and ask the child to guess the identity of his secret admirer.

Your secret admirer is wearing a blue sweater.

Apples, bananas, peaches, a pear,
Can you guess who I am
By the clothes that I wear?

Heart to Heart

In *Heart to Heart* by George Shannon (Houghton Mifflin Company), Squirrel gives Mole a valentine made with memorabilia from special times they spent together. Invite your youngsters to collect memorabilia from a special day spent with friends. Divide the class into pairs. Encourage each pair of valentine pals to stay together throughout the day. Give them a large resealable plastic bag with their names on it. Encourage them to collect a token from each activity they engage in together, such as a small block, an art material, a puzzle piece, a book, or a dress-up item. At the end of the day, have each set of valentine pals share the contents of their bag with the class and recall the fun they had together.

Franklin's Valentines

Touch your youngsters' hearts with a reading of *Franklin's Valentines* by Paulette Bourgeois and Sharon Jennings (Cartwheel Books). Franklin and his classmates celebrate the meaning of true friendship at their valentine party. Celebrate in the same way with your little friends, and make these turtle cupcakes as a delicious party treat. In advance, prepare the following for each child: one mini cupcake, a tablespoon of white frosting tinted with green food coloring, a green Gummy Worm® cut into four 1-inch pieces, one green gumdrop, and one half of a walnut shell (with the nut removed). Place the items on a paper plate, along with a craft stick.

After reading the story to the class, discuss how Franklin learned from his friends a lesson in giving. Then invite each child to make a Franklin cupcake to give to a friend. Have her use a craft stick to spread the frosting onto her cupcake. Have her place the walnut shell half on the frosted cupcake to resemble Franklin's shell. Next have her add a gumdrop head and Gummy Worm arms and legs. Encourage your little ones to exchange cupcakes in the name of friendship. (Be sure youngsters remove the walnut shell halves before munching their party treats!)

The Valentine Bears

Eve Bunting's *The Valentine Bears* (Clarion Books) is a story that "bears" rereading! As a fun follow-up, invite youngsters to make a sign like the lovely one Mrs. Bear made for Mr. Bear. Write "It's Nice to Share Valentine's Day With Someone You Love" inside a heart-shaped outline. Make a photocopy on red construction paper for each child. Have each child cut out a heart and glue it to a sheet of 12" x 18" white construction paper. Provide valentine art supplies, such as heart-shaped stickers and stamps, red and white yarn, red and silver glitter, and paper doilies. Encourage each youngster to put her heart into decorating her sign. When the finishing touches are complete, have her roll it up and tie it with red curling ribbon to take home to her loved ones.

Community

A Delivery of ABCs and 123s

Send some letter- and number-matching skills your students' way with this post office center. To prepare, purchase a cardboard shoe organizer to serve as a set of mailboxes. (Or ask a grocer to donate boxes with cardboard dividers.) Label each compartment with a different child's name and a number. Label a variety of envelopes with corresponding student names and mailbox numbers. Put the envelopes in a tote bag. Then invite each of your little letter carriers, in turn, to deliver each labeled envelope to the appropriate mailbox. To extend the activity, invite each child to write a letter to a classmate. Then help her copy the classmate's name and mailbox number onto an envelope. Have the child seal the letter in the envelope, then put it in the bag for a future delivery.

Community Helpers Count

Encourage youngsters to combine counting and social studies with these booklets. To begin, duplicate page 207 for each child. Help youngsters identify the workers shown on the pages. Then have each child count the community helpers on each page and write the corresponding number on the provided line. (You might supply number stamps for younger children to use.) Then ask the child to color and cut out each page. Help her sequence her pictures behind her cover page, then staple her booklet together. Invite each child to read her book to several adults and classmates before she takes it home to share with her family.

POLICE LINE

3 _____ police officers

Helpers

teaches us to count
sings songs

Charles
Danielle
Jamie

puts out fires
wears a raincoat

Ben   Luke
Rodney   Gray
Kenny

brings us mail

Dane
Caroline

When I Grow Up

Which community helpers do your little ones want to be when they grow up? Find out with this language activity that explores job roles. Copy page 207; then cut the boxes apart. Glue each box to the top of a separate sheet of chart paper; then display the charts on a chalkboard. Have youngsters identify the community helpers in the pictures. Then encourage them to share what they know about each occupation. Write their responses on the corresponding chart. Next, review the information on the charts; then discuss the advantages and challenges of each job. Finally, have each youngster write his name on the chart showing the job he would most enjoy. As a class, count the names on each chart. Then compare the findings to discover the most desired job of your class.

Community Helpers in Song

Strengthen language skills while singing the praises of our community helpers. To prepare, write "firefighter" and "police officer" on separate sentence strips. Challenge older youngsters to use their knowledge of beginning sounds to figure out these words. Then teach your class this song about these two important community helpers. Insert the name of your city in the blank. Then, while singing, hold up the sentence strip corresponding to the named community helper. Afterward, encourage students to create new verses about other community helpers.

*(sung to the tune of
"Mary Had a Little Lamb")*

[Phoenix] has firefighters,
Firefighters, firefighters.
[Phoenix] has firefighters
To put the fires out.

[Phoenix] has police officers,
Police officers, police officers.
[Phoenix] has police officers
To keep our city safe.

Helper Math

Do your students need help solving math problems? Community helpers to the rescue! Invite a small group of children to build a city from wooden, foam, or LEGO® blocks. Then give the group a set of toy people figures. State a simple word problem featuring community helpers. For example, you might say "Two police officers were standing by the station. One more officer joined them. How many police officers are there now?" Encourage youngsters to discover the solution by acting out the problem with figures.

Caroline wants to be a nurse when she grows up so she can help sick people get better.

Future Careers

What does the future hold for each of your students? Invite them to share their vision at the art center! In advance, gather lots of images of working people—from magazine pictures, books, or clip art; then put these in a basket in your art center. Invite each child who visits the center to browse through the pictures, then select one that she envisions for herself. Encourage her to draw a picture of herself as her chosen worker. Write each child's dictation about her career on her paper. Display the drawings in your classroom.

Letter-Perfect Career Choices

Encourage your little ones to spell out their career choices with this tip-top center activity. To prepare, gather a collection of dress-up hats or ask parents to donate or lend hats associated with various careers. Display the hats near a full-length mirror in your dramatic-play center. Invite youngsters to don the different hats; then take an instant photo of each child in the hat of his choice. In the space below the photo, use a permanent marker to write the occupation associated with the hat. Then place the photos, a cookie sheet, and a basket of magnetic letters in a center. Challenge students to use the letters to spell out the occupations written on the photos.

FIREFIGHTER

Helpers

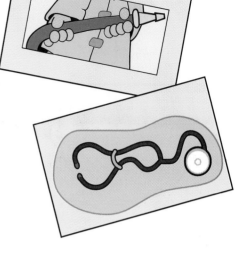

Tool Time

Set up a building center for your budding architects and carpenters. To begin, gather a supply of golf tees, wooden blocks, plastic knives, and large pieces of Styrofoam® packaging to place in a center. Then invite your builders to create structures using the Styrofoam® building material, wooden-block hammers, golf-tee nails, and plastic-knife saws. Just watch the enthusiasm build at this center designed for fun!

Career Categories

Set up a center to expose your students to all sorts of jobs. Cut out magazine and catalog pictures representing workers, tools, and clothing associated with different jobs. Glue each cutout onto a separate tagboard card. Put the cards in a center; then encourage each little worker to sort the cards according to the related jobs. For an added challenge, have the child sort the cards into three groups—workers, tools, and career clothing. Then compliment the child on a job well done!

Construction Zone

Are there some future construction workers in your group? Provide them with props to turn your dramatic-play center into a construction zone! In advance, collect a few children's belts to transform into tool belts. To make a tool belt, cut a set of plastic six-pack rings in half lengthwise. Weave a belt in and out of one half (three rings); then hot-glue or staple the rings securely to the belt. Plastic toy tools can be slipped into the open spaces between the belt and the rings. Place the tool belts and other construction accessories—such as toy tools and dress-up hard hats—in your dramatic-play center.

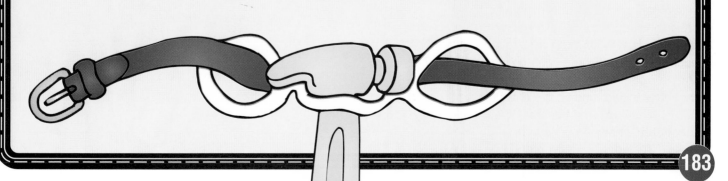

U.S. Community

Kenny B.

The Mail Carrier Always Delivers

Help your students improve their letter-identification skills with this first-class idea. To prepare, write each child's first name on the front of a separate envelope. Inside each envelope, put a single magnetic letter or a slip of paper with a letter of the alphabet written on it. Put the envelopes inside a backpack or tote. Invite a child to role-play a mail carrier, and help him deliver the mail to each child. Encourage each youngster to open his envelope, identify the letter inside, and give a child's name or a word that begins with that letter. That's fun—signed, sealed, and delivered!

Weather Watchers

"Weather" or not it's cold outside, this weather song will heat things up at circle time. To prepare, color and cut out the weather pictures on page 197; then laminate them for durability. Hot-glue each picture to a separate dowel or ruler. Write the words to the following song on chart paper, leaving a blank in the third line. Each day, invite a child to be the weather reporter. Have him select the appropriate weather stick for the day and use it to point to the words of the song as the class sings along. Cue youngsters to fill in the appropriate weather term in the third line.

Zip-a-Dee-Doo-Dah Weather
(sung to the tune of "Zip-a-Dee-Doo-Dah")

Zip-a-dee-doo-dah—
    zip-a-dee-day,
My, oh my, what's the weather
    today?
Plenty of [sunshine]
    heading our way.
Zip-a-dee-doo-dah—
    zip-a-dee-day.

Helpers

Dressed for Success

Dress up your show-and-tell time by inviting your youngsters to wear career-specific clothing. Encourage each child—on a specified day—to come to school dressed in the type of clothes that his mom, his dad, or a selected community helper wears to work. Ask parents to help their child find appropriate props and rehearse a description of the job for which he is dressed. Heigh-ho! Heigh-ho! It's off to work they go!

Undercover Careers

Uncover the careers of our community helpers with this mystery box. To prepare, collect items that indicate certain types of work, such as a firefighter's hat, a hammer, a stethoscope, or a whistle. Cover a box and its lid separately with Con-Tact® paper. Each day, secretly place one career item in the mystery box. Describe the item at circle time; then challenge the children to guess what it is and who uses it before revealing the undercover item.

Career Song

Help your youngsters describe some community helpers' jobs with this catchy career song.

Community Capers
(sung to the tune of "The Itsy-Bitsy Spider")
There are [firefighters] in our community.
They [put out fires] and they help you and me.

They're always there when there's a job to do.
So when you see a [firefighter], be sure to say, "Thank you!"

Repeat the song as many times as desired, substituting the careers and phrases below, or others your youngsters come up with.

police officers...direct the traffic
doctors...make us well
postal workers...deliver mail
farmers...grow our food

Busy Bakers

No "knead" to worry about how to cook up some fun in your classroom—simply follow this recipe for a fine-motor workout. To prepare, gather cookie cutters, cookie sheets, a rolling pin, waxed paper, baker's hats, and aprons. Then invite a group of youngsters to help you mix a batch of baker's clay. Encourage them to help with measuring and pouring the ingredients, then to take turns mixing the dough with their hands. (Once the dough gets very stiff, finish the mixing yourself.) Then place the clay on a table dusted with flour. Give each child a portion of the clay with which to experiment. Invite your little bakers to create cookies from the clay. Place each child's cookie on a cookie sheet; then bake them at 250°F for two hours. (Or allow them to air-dry for several days.) After the cookies cool, invite youngsters to paint them with tempera paint. If desired, spray a coat of clear acrylic on the cookies; then use them as play food in your housekeeping area.

Baker's Clay
(enough for 10–12 children)

4 cups all-purpose flour
1 1/2 cups water
1 cup salt

Mix the ingredients by hand in a large bowl. Add water or flour as needed until the dough is pliable, but not wet.

Locksmith's Station

Your little apprentices will discover the keys for unlocking fun at this locksmith's station. Set up a center with a variety of items containing locks and corresponding keys, such as padlocks, diaries, jewelry boxes, briefcases, small suitcases, and lockboxes. Put the keys in a small basket. Then encourage each child to find the key that opens each lock. Then have the apprentice relock each item and return the keys to the basket so that the next locksmith can start his shift.

Helpers

Junior Chefs

Fine-motor skills will be at their finest when your young chefs prepare the special of the day—fresh fruit salad. In advance, ask each child to bring to school a fruit that can be chopped into pieces, such as an apple, a banana, a pear, or a tangerine. Set up a center with a cutting board, a large mixing bowl, and plastic knives. Pour a can of pineapple tidbits with juice into the bowl. (The pineapple juice will keep the cut fruits from turning brown too quickly.) Prepare the donated fruit by cutting apples and pears into strips (discarding the cores and seeds) and peeling away a small portion of each tangerine.

Remind little ones to wash their hands thoroughly before visiting this supervised center, where they can peel or chop fruit for a fruit salad. Have each chef add chopped pieces to the bowl. Periodically coat the fruit with the pineapple juice. After each child has added some fruit to the bowl, serve the finished fruit salad at snacktime. Mmmmm!

Nuts and Bolts

This construction zone is pegged for excitement! In advance, collect several thick foam pegboards with large holes. Take the pegboards to your local hardware store to find and purchase blunt-tip bolts that fit snugly into the holes without harming the board. Buy a nut for each bolt. (You may want to purchase wing nuts to use

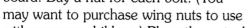

with younger children.) Place the nuts, bolts, and pegboards in a center. Invite each of your construction workers to gently push a bolt into a pegboard hole and then screw a nut onto the bolt. If desired, provide a wrench for those construction workers who might enjoy an added challenge. After a child fills her pegboard with bolts and nuts, have her remove them to prepare the center for the next group of workers.

House Painting Made Easy

Invite youngsters to paint the town—or at least a house or two! Obtain from your local paint store some inexpensive props, such as painter's hats, buckets, paint rollers, paintbrushes, and paint stirrers. Set up your chalkboard as a painting area. Place a drop cloth on the floor beneath the chalkboard to catch any drips. Put the paintbrushes and rollers, along with buckets of water to represent paint, on the drop cloth. Then encourage each painter to draw a chalk outline of a large house or building on the chalkboard. Have him carefully "paint" his building with a brush or roller, trying to stay within the chalk lines. Allow time for the "paint" to dry. Then erase the chalkboard before the next paint crew reports for duty.

U.S.

5

Community

P.E. and Me!

Encourage your little athletes to play the role of the physical education teacher! Select one child each day to wear a whistle and lead the class in opening exercises such as knee bends, toe touches, and arm circles. Count to ten with each exercise. Now, that's a community helper role that physically fits the part!

Helpers on the Go

Take dramatic play outdoors and let riding toys add to the fun! Ready a box of the suggested props below for role-playing various community helpers. Then gather all your riding toys to transform into "helper-mobiles." Have a few students at a time select career roles. Help those youngsters choose appropriate props and vehicles to assist them in their roles. Heigh-ho! Heigh-ho! It's off to work they go!

Careers	Riding Toys	Props
police officer	trike, scooter	police officer's cap, pad and pencil to write tickets
medic	wagon	nurse's hat, ambulance sign
mail carrier	trike, wagon	mail carrier's hat, empty envelopes, wooden blocks to represent packages
grocery deliverer	trike, wagon	plastic foods from housekeeping center, collection of cardboard food boxes

Helpers

Pizza Delivery

Serve up some fun with this version of Drop the Handkerchief. Bring in an empty pizza box or use a heavy paper plate as a pizza. Choose one child to be the pizza delivery person. Have the rest of the class (the customers) sit in a circle and sing the following song:

(sung to the tune of "A-Tisket, A-Tasket")

> A pizza, a pizza.
> A pepperoni pizza.
> Ordered a pizza for my friend,
> And then had it delivered.
> Delivered, delivered.
> Then had it delivered.

As the class sings, direct the delivery person to walk around the outside of the circle carrying the pizza prop. When the song ends, have her stand behind the customer of her choice and say, "Ding-dong." Then have her drop the pizza and run around the circle as the customer chases her. She should try to reach the customer's spot in the circle without being tagged. If she is tagged, she must go to the center of the circle—the pizzeria—until another child replaces her. Invite the customer to become the pizza delivery person for the next round.

Community Charades

Play this game of career charades to help your little ones identify workers from all walks of life. First demonstrate how to pantomime the actions of a desired community helper. Actions might include a police officer directing traffic, a firefighter using a hose, or a doctor examining a patient. Can your youngsters guess who you are portraying? After your demonstration, ask for volunteers to pantomime other careers for the class. This type of fun may be just what the doctor ordered!

On the Move

Over the long haul, this loading and unloading activity will be a favorite with your little movers and shakers! Gather three wagons and several of the following loading items: large wooden blocks, small cardboard boxes, or soda bottles filled with water. Talk about people whose jobs require loading and unloading—such as grocery baggers, movers, and dockhands.

Then bring your youngsters outdoors, and divide the class into three teams, with one designated truck driver per team. Have one-half of each team stand behind a marked starting line, while the other half stands behind a finish line. At the starting line provide a wagon and an equal number of loading items for each team. Blow a whistle, and instruct each team to load its wagon. The truck driver must bring the loaded wagon to his team at the finish line, where they must unload the items before the quitting-time whistle blows!

Community Helpers

Hammer and Nails

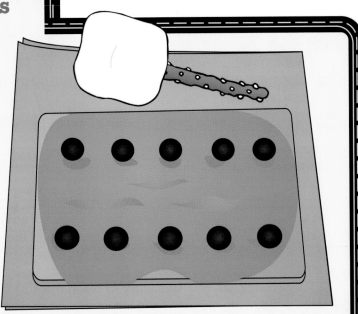

Ingredients:
1 graham cracker per child
peanut butter
1 large marshmallow per child
1 pretzel stick per child
chocolate chips

Utensils and Supplies:
1 plastic knife (or craft stick) per child
napkins

Teacher Preparation:
   Arrange the ingredients and utensils near the step-by-step direction cards.

What to Do When the Snack Is Through

   Explain to youngsters that ants live together in a community, with each ant having a job to do to help its community. Many ants have the job of gathering food, and your little ones can watch these workers in action! Search your school or center grounds for an anthill; then place a large plastic hoop around it. Along the inside of the hoop, spread a few leftover pretzels, marshmallows, and chocolate chips. Have students stand around the hoop. Caution youngsters not to touch the food or the ants. Stand back and observe the ants go marching one by one to work!

Peanut Butter

spread

3

hammer!

6

©The Education Center, Inc. • Busy Kids® Busy Days—Fall & Winter • TEC546

put

2

push in

5

Hammer and Nails

wash

1

count 10

4

U.S.

Community

Thank You, Mr. Postman

(sung to the tune of "Jingle Bells")

I got mail!
I got mail!
I got mail today!
Thank you, Mr. Postman, for bringing mail
  my way!

I got mail!
I got mail!
I got mail today!
Thank you, Mr. Postman, you've brightened up
  my day!

Here's a kiss for you, Lizzy.

My Teacher Loves Me

Sing this song to let your youngsters know how much you care for them. Then give each child a chocolate kiss or heart sticker as a symbol of your heartfelt love.

(sung to the tune of "Jesus Loves Me")

My teacher loves me,
This I know.
In many ways (s)he
Shows me so.
Teaching me to read and write,
Helping me learn wrong from right.
Yes, my teacher loves me.
Yes, my teacher loves me.
Yes, my teacher loves me.
In, oh, so many ways.

Helpers

The Little Fire Station

One little fire station
   closed up tight.
Ten snoring firefighters
   sleep away the night.
"Ding, ding, ding!" Hear
   the fire bell shout!
Ten firefighters jump up
   to put the fire out!

Clasp hands with fingers inside.

Make snoring sound.

Shake clasped hands.

Open hands and wiggle fingers.

People We Can Trust

Teach youngsters this song to reinforce the importance of trusting community helpers. Each time you sing the song, replace the underlined word with a different community helper, such as *police officer, doctor, teacher,* or *school nurse.*

(sung to the tune of "Are You Sleeping?")

Who can you trust?
Who can you trust?
Who's your friend?
Who's your friend?
You can trust a [firefighter].
You can trust a [firefighter].
To be your friend.
To be your friend.

Our Sunny Meteorologist

During your study of community helpers, assign a different child each day to be the class meteorologist. Then have her report the weather after the class sings this song.

(sung to the tune of "Row, Row, Row Your Boat")

Sun, wind, rain, or snow?
What will come our way?
Let's ask the meteorologist
About the weather today.

sunny

193

Hounds Around Town:
A Guess-What-They-Do Flap Book

Youngsters will be hounding you to read Megan Halsey's *Hounds Around Town* (Little Simon) over and over again. As you read the story, invite children to lift the flaps to reveal hidden community helpers busy at work. After completing the story, teach the class the following song. Then sing the song together as you browse through the pages of the book. Instead of reading the text again, invite youngsters to name the community helpers they see on each page and give a description of each helper's job. Can they recall who is working behind each flap by looking at the setting for clues? Replace "Houndtown" in the following song with the words "our town," and sing it anytime to review community helpers and their important jobs.

(sung to the tune of "This Old Man")

In Houndtown
All around,
There are helpers to be found.
Let's try to name them one by one.
What are the jobs they must get done?

Who Uses This?

As you study community helpers, hammer home the tools of the trades with a reading of *Who Uses This?* by Margaret Miller (Mulberry Books). After sharing the book, gather pictures of community helpers and collect various tools used by them, such as a police officer's badge, a teacher's chalk, and a chef's mixing bowl and spoon. Display the community helpers with the wrong tool placed in front of each helper. Have youngsters match the correct tool to each community helper and ask them to name other tools that might be used by each one. Later, place the tools in your dramatic-play center and invite your little ones to role-play the duties of each job.

194

Helpers

Firehouse Dog

Read *Firehouse Dog* by Amy and Richard Hutchings (Cartwheel Books) and introduce your students to a dalmatian named Hooper. After learning about the lives of a fireman and a firehouse dog, invite youngsters to visit Hooper at the "station"—your classroom math station, that is! Draw a simple pattern of a dog wearing a collar; then duplicate a desired number on white construction paper. Laminate the copies for durability. Program each dog with a numeral on its collar, and then place the programmed cutouts at a center. To complete this center, a child uses a black wipe-off marker to draw spots on each dog to match the numerals on the dog collars. If desired, program the dalmatians to reinforce other skills, such as matching upper- and lowercase letters or matching consonant sounds and pictures. There's a lot to be learned from Hooper!

A Carpenter

Your youngsters will see how a carpenter works with wood in Douglas Florian's *A Carpenter* (Greenwillow Books). Try this follow-up activity to help your students build their knowledge. In advance write the word *wood* on several index cards. After reading the book, have children use the index cards to label wooden items in your classroom. Remind them that a carpenter or woodworker made all the wooden items they find—from floors and doors to puzzles and toys! As youngsters search for wooden items, help them identify items they find that are made from other materials, such as glass, metal, or plastic—all made by busy community helpers!

Trashy Town

After seeing Mr. Gilly pick up trash all over Trashy Town, your youngsters will have a new appreciation for hardworking sanitation workers. So extend a reading of *Trashy Town* by Andrea Zimmerman and David Clemesha (HarperCollins Publishers) by having your class send a great big thank-you note to your town's sanitation workers. To prepare, write a message (as shown) in large letters on a sheet of poster board. Next, cut a few kitchen sponges into trashcan shapes (rectangles with rounded short sides). Then set up a painting station with the poster board, the sponges, a shallow container of silver tempera paint, and black markers. Have each child sponge-paint a silver trash can on the poster. When the paint dries, have her add details to her trash can (as shown) with a black marker and then sign her name below it. Arrange to have the thank-you poster delivered to your town's sanitation department, or leave it at your school's dumpster.

You dump it in;
You smash it down.
Thanks for cleaning up
Our trashy town!

Thanks from
Mrs. Flagg's Kindergarten
Apache Elementary

Leaf Lotto Board

Use with "Leaf Match" on page 23.

©The Education Center, Inc. • *Busy Kids® Busy Days—Fall & Winter* • TEC546

Leaf Pictures
Use with "Leaves in Action"
on page 24 and "Problems
With Leaves" on page 25.

Climbing Jack
Use with "A Fine Vine" on page 84.

Bat Pattern
Use with "Bat Match" on page 53.

©The Education Center, Inc. • *Busy Kids® Busy Days—Fall & Winter* • TEC546

Bat Pattern
Use with "Vanishing Bat Act" on page 59.

Turkey Pattern
Use with "A Flock of Fringed Feathers" and "Our Fine-Feathered Friends" on page 74 and "Terrific Turkey Tails" on page 75.

Cornucopia Patterns
Use with "Cornucopia Counting" on page 68.

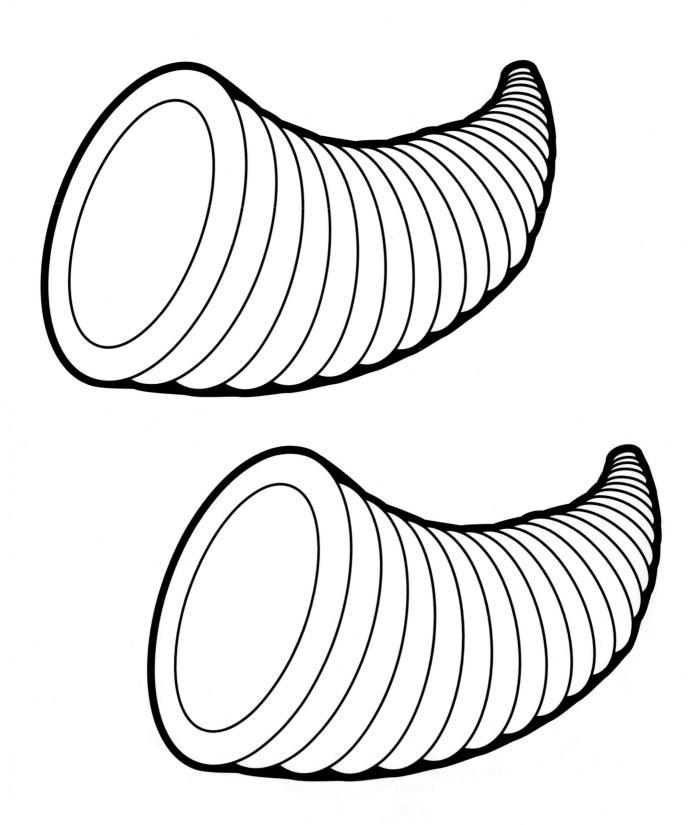

©The Education Center, Inc. • *Busy Kids® Busy Days—Fall & Winter* • TEC546

©The Education Center, Inc. • *Busy Kids® Busy Days—Fall & Winter* • TEC546

Paper-Doll Pattern
Use with "Paper-Doll Pals" on page 102.

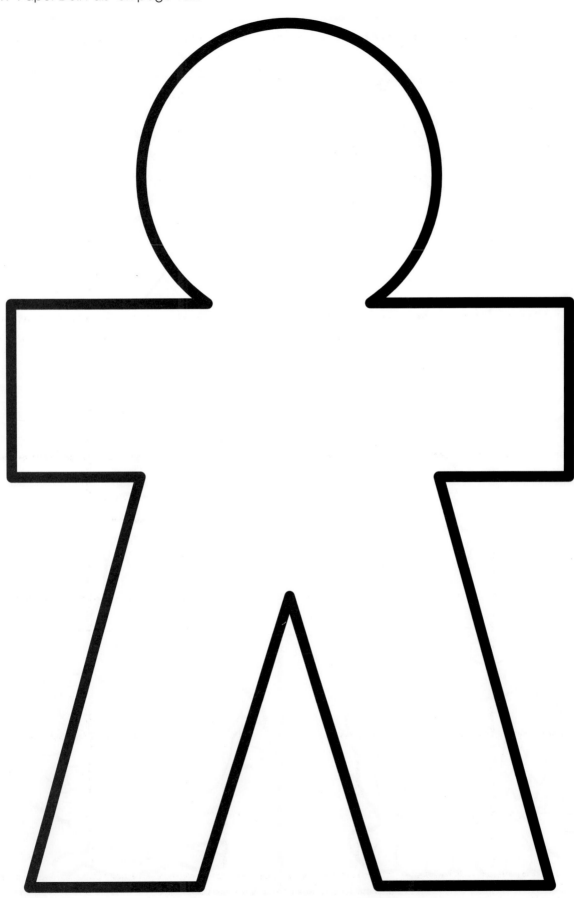

©The Education Center, Inc. • *Busy Kids® Busy Days—Fall & Winter* • TEC546

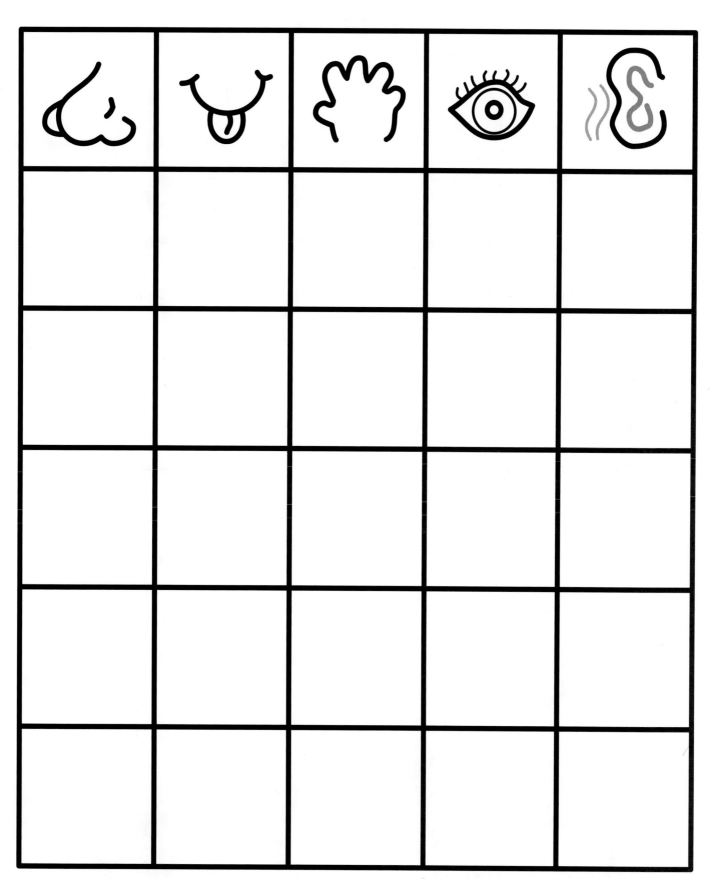

Note to the teacher: Use with "Another 'Sense-ational' Idea" on page 131.

Reindeer and Carrot Patterns
Use with *Where's Prancer?*
on page 147.

©The Education Center, Inc. • *Busy Kids® Busy Days—Fall & Winter* • TEC546

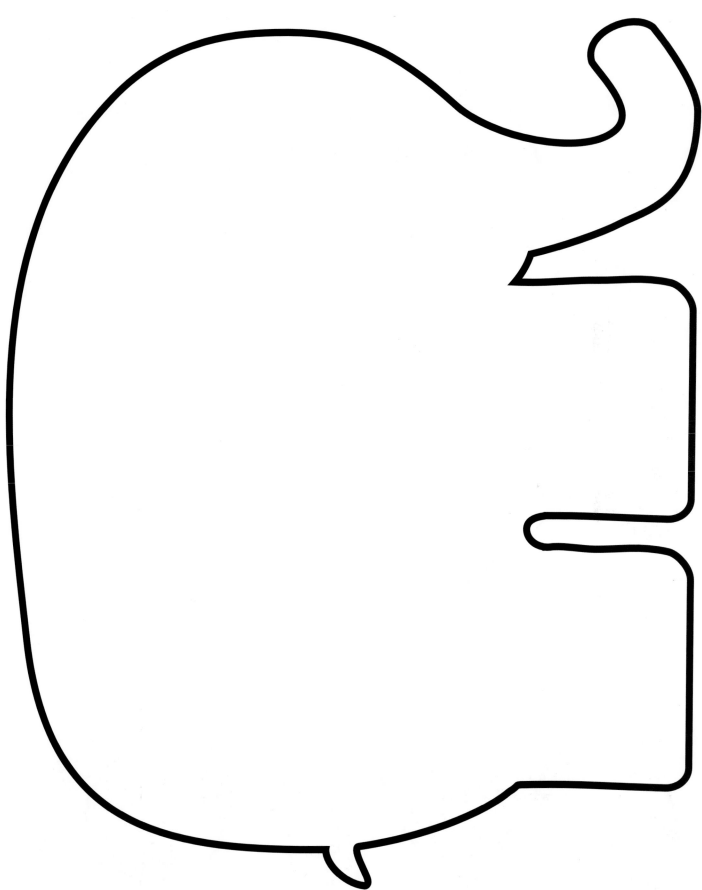

Heart Patterns

Use with "Valentine Finger Folly" on page 171.

©The Education Center, Inc. • *Busy Kids® Busy Days—Fall & Winter* • TEC546

mail carrier

police officers

POLICE L

firefighters

You Can Count On Community Helpers

©The Education Center, Inc.

A B C

teachers

nurses

Managing Editor: Scott Lyons
Contributing Editors: Jayne M. Gammons, Ada Goren, Kim T. Griswell, Mackie Rhodes
Contributing Writers: Jan Brennan, LeeAnn Collins, Ann Flagg, Lisa Leonardi, Dayle Timmons
Copy Editors: Sylvan Allen, Karen Brewer Grossman, Amy Kirtley-Hill, Karen L. Huffman, Debbie Shoffner
Cover Artist: Clevell Harris
Artists: Nick Greenwood, Susan Hodnett, Rebecca Saunders
Contributing Artist: Cathy Spangler Bruce
Typesetters: Lynette Dickerson, Mark Rainey

President, The Mailbox Book Company™: Joseph C. Bucci
Director of Book Planning and Development: Chris Poindexter
Book Development Managers: Elizabeth H. Lindsay, Thad McLaurin, Susan Walker
Curriculum Director: Karen P. Shelton
Traffic Manager: Lisa K. Pitts
Librarian: Dorothy C. McKinney
Editorial and Freelance Management: Karen A. Brudnak
Editorial Training: Irving P. Crump
Editorial Assistants: Terrie Head, Hope Rodgers, Jan E. Witcher

www.themailbox.com